TENNIS AND
AMERICA,
THANK YOU

Memoirs of a Czech Refugee, 1948

FREDDIE BOTUR

authorHOUSE®

AuthorHouse™
1663 Liberty Drive
Bloomington, IN 47403
www.authorhouse.com
Phone: 1 (800) 839-8640

Published by AuthorHouse 05/22/2018

ISBN: 978-1-4817-4684-7 (sc)
ISBN: 978-1-4817-4683-0 (hc)
ISBN: 978-1-4817-4685-4 (e)

Library of Congress Control Number: 2013909057

Print information available on the last page.

Contents

Chapter Three: "Mister, Do You Play Tennis?" The question which changed my life forever in 1948. 64

Chapter Four: Not Enough Tennis Clubs in New York 88

Chapter Six: Successful: Tennis Inc in Armory on 34th St, West Park Racquet Club on 97th St and Columbus Ave, Tennis 59th St Under the bridge, Cedarhurst Tennis Club and the Eminent Domain of Tennisport Inc in Queens 174

Prologue

There shouldn't have been anything special about that flight in 1965. It was one of those hops that carry millions of people across short distances every day. You board, taxi down the runway, take off, and you ritualistically check your watch for the two-minute mark that you believe means you're safe. The plane gains altitude, and, before you know it, you hear the wheels descend, preparing for landing.

How many times I have taken those short flights, I cannot count,—a routine run between a place I am leaving and one I am going to. But calmness and sleep eluded me that night. I stared out the window, transfixed by a forest of skyscrapers twinkling with warm yellow from inside buildings and red aviatic warning lights on roof poles. Millions of glowing windows along endless stretches and plains of suburbia were interwoven with endless highways flooded with cars, dashing downtown or rushing to escape it.

I knew the source of my restlessness. *Sit down and write.* I was listening to a city. Worse yet, I was about to obey its instructions to write, orders that would consume a good part of my life over the next five years and that were no easy task. I am not, you see, a writer.

But there was Chicago confronting me, pinning me down— Chicago, where an artist named Chiang Er-Shih and his wife befriended my wife and me and manipulated their way, by accident or design, deep into our lives and hearts before taking us for a ride that nearly cost us everything we had. Er-Shih was as brilliant an artist as he was a con artist. And yet, upon his death many years later, I found myself forgiving him. His bizarre story and our friendship was but one of dozens of tales that together formed the fabric of lives so rich that its many vignettes and stories are itching to be told. Here was Chicago, where my distant relatives were from, the relatives who were, the first persons I had ever met outside my village in Czechoslovakia. The relatives who, with one brief afternoon visit, wandered into my life and out again and for the first time made me understand there were places outside my neighborhood.

First, there is something else you should know besides the fact that I am not a writer. I have never been especially sentimental, nor have I had any particular inclination to look back. And I have never had either the time or an urge to philosophize. I am single-minded. Call it straight-ahead vision, aimed forward, not past. I ponder what is going to be, rarely bothering to compare it to what was, though I have to confess that things change when you reach ninety; there is a little more self-indulgence in reflection.

I sank deep into my seat, closed my eyes, and tilted my head back. My wife, Annegret, who was traveling with me, probably thought I was sleeping. And though sitting so close that our arms were comfortably touching, I was thousands of miles away. My mind was in another country on another continent long ago. As the plane pushed on, leaving miles behind, my thoughts flew with equal force in reverse, back to an age and place when flight was the prerogative of birds, not machines, and the sense of urgency was about reaching a land of freedom, not getting to the nearest tournament, event, or deal. It is not so much that our lives are easier or harder, simpler or more complicated, more or less worthy; it is just that they are different. I have seen both sides through nine decades of love, sorrow, war, success, and defeat. I have become some of the things I would have expected had I given it a thought—a husband, father, and grandfather—and some of what I never could have planned: a successful entrepreneur, a rancher, and a fighter taking on the City of New York in an eminent domain arena for a decade. Most of all, I have become a survivor for many decades who has tried to help others.

When the pictures started flowing through my mind, they swept me along, beginning with childhood innocence in Mistek, Czechoslovakia, when I was playing in fields and streams in summer and skiing mountains and skating on a frozen lake in winter. I recalled plentiful food on the table, my uncle's mischievous ways, my mother's soft voice, and then the war and my stern father glued to the oversized brown radio as if he could urge good news out of it. He had a look in his eyes that I had never seen before. I now understand that he knew what was coming before it arrived—first Nazi dictatorship and then the communist coup the end of democracy and life as we knew it, which would be severed, sliced off as cleanly as a chopping knife slices fat from lean.

In 1948 fearing for my life, with my parents approval a young man of twenty six, I fled the communist occupation, scared and at times falling asleep with a gun by my side and hunger in my belly, which hurt due to its emptiness. I moved through war-torn Europe, horrified. Frankfurt was destitute, flattened by bombing, and occupied by Allied armies. I was just one more refugee lost in a continent of displaced persons trying to survive, seeing a land shattered by war—physically, emotionally, politically, and morally. Finally, I found a place to stay and started recruiting for the Allies, dodging the enemy and working the underground. Later I married and moved again and again, first to Australia, where my odds were far better than in the refugee camps of Europe, but the welcome was barely skin deep. A few years later, I moved again, this time to America, a country swarming with immigrants and refugees. There, my wife and I were just ordinary citizens with more hope than luggage, and we had just as much of a chance as anyone else. There were so many years to remember, so many memories to recall. Why I dwelt in the distant past that night on the plane I have no idea. It was the most recent past that was more important.

The plane bounced ever so slightly. I looked over at Annegret and was again filled with wonder, as I had been so many times over the years, this creature of energy, beauty and kindness had come into my life, mothered our children, started new American generation, inspired our grandchildren, befriended more strangers than anyone I had ever known, and made them friends forever. I smiled, and she moved just a tiny bit in her seat, settling down a little closer to my shoulder. In the quiet, I slipped back into my reverie for a few more precious moments, to prewar life, a time when people used kerosene lamps for light and radio was novel, when a horse-drawn wagon ride was transportation and not an exotic holiday experience, and when a car ride earned you a special social status in the village for life. In my mind, I traveled to the small town in the Beskydy Mountains where I had been born one biting cold February night ninety years ago. The village was the only world I knew until one summer day when I was about ten a four-cylinder, hardtop Whippet stopped in front of our modest house. My grandmother's small convenience store, which was part of the house, had never attracted more than foot or horse-drawn traffic, so everyone in the village gathered and gawked, all eyes staring as if a space ship had landed. Two elderly couples emerged (or so they seemed to a young boy, to whom anyone over thirty was elderly).

They were followed by two pretty ladies in long dark dresses with hats and white gloves, the Knezeks from Chicago. My grandparents came out and welcomed them to the house, and they said that they were going to visit my grandma's relatives in Vienna and combine the trip by visiting us with a big detour to our village Mistek, which my grandparents appreciated. To this day, the sight of them remains stunningly vivid in my mind.

But the story begins even earlier than the visit from the ladies in gloves from that distant place called America. It begins in a small town in Sviadnov, Moravia, a part of Czechoslovakia, on a night so cold that people's breath froze in midair.

Chapter One

Vratislav

None of us pick our own name, but others picked my name twice. The name given to me by my parents at birth, Vratislav, served me well in what was then Czechoslovakia. Fate intervened and I was destined to spend the majority of my life in a country where my name was almost unpronounceable.

The second involuntary naming happened in New York City around 1954, when I was introducing myself to a River Club member signing up for a tennis lesson. Mr. Webster, an older gentleman, did not understand me when I said, "My name is Vratislav Botur." I cannot blame his inability to pronounce Vratislav on his age or his hearing. It had happened often in the United States and earlier in Australia. In New York City, I had to not only repeat it but spell it many times over and with a thick accent. It was always trying. When Mr Webster at the River Club asked me to spell my name, I started slowly saying the letters—V-R-A-T—and before I had the chance to finish, he stopped me. Because of my thick accent or maybe his hearing, or maybe because Fred Perry was a hot name in tennis at the time, he decided to call me Fred. "Fred," he said loudly, and I replied, "Yes, sir." That was it. I said yes, because I thought it would be much simpler. I have to thank Mr. Webster because, since then, I haven't had to spell Vratislav much. So unlike most, I was named by others not once, but twice. Since then I have been using Freddie V. Botur for business purposes, which was very useful after the war in Germany because they thought that the middle initial V., could be mistakenly understood to stand for Von.

Winters were hard and long for the people living in villages of the Beskydy Mountains, but my family told me that the winter of my birth, 1922, was even colder than usual for a region all too

1

familiar with months of deep, bone-numbing chill. People knew what the bitterness and cold meant. They prepared by stocking up on coal, wood, and potatoes before they were isolated by the winter snows. Electricity at the beginning of the 20th Century had not made its way from places like Italy and Switzerland to the mountains and villages of Czechoslovakia yet. Once daylight faded, petrol lamps gave off what light there was and coal and wood stoves provided heat. When my mother was pregnant with me, she made sure to have the midwife ready and nearby. Like most babies then, at that time, I was born at home, at my grandparents' house, with a midwife and no doctor. Mother told me I was fortunate before even being born. When she was six months pregnant, she was riding with my Father in a carriage when the horse bolted, sending the carriage careening into a ditch, where it overturned, an early indication that my life would be anything but a straight road. She feared a miscarriage, but instead she had a healthy baby boy. At the time it was considered fortunate to have a boy.

I never knew how my parents met. Perhaps it was in Vienna when my father was the manager of the largest and busiest meatpacking facility in the city. Perhaps my mother, a violinist, was playing with the philharmonic there or visiting her grandmother in suburban Neusiedel in Vienna and they had recalled each other from Mistek.

In today's world, they would have been unlikely to be compatible on Match.com, but life was very different almost a century ago.

The stern, good-looking meat packer and the romantic violinist married and moved in to my mother's parents' home in Mistek, where my dad opened a butcher shop nearby. What I learned under his tutelage, though often delivered with more than a touch of military discipline, would help save my life later, but that is a story for another time as well. His brother, my uncle Alfred, had a restaurant in the town square. As a boy, I often stayed with Uncle Alfred and helped in the restaurant, where I was most frequently assigned the inglorious task of peeling potatoes. It was an experience that gave me more courage than skill as I discovered later when, desperate for a job, I brazenly called myself a cook and talked a employment official into hiring me, a decision that it did not take them long to regret—or reverse.

Our village was Sviadnov, a few kilometers from Mistek, a town of about twenty thousand in the northeast of Moravia, near Ostrava, the third-largest city in Czechoslovakia with many coal mines and steel mills. It borders Poland, Slovakia, and Germany and was vulnerable to annexation first by the Nazis and later small area by the Polish. To this day, Mistek haunts my boys memories with its mountain views and the beauty of its countryside. Because of its fragile history and accident of geography, it became a pawn in a game it watched and over which it had little control.

Until 1918, four years before I was born, Moravia, Bohemia, Slovakia, and a corner of the Ukraine had all been part of the Austrian-Hungarian Empire for three centuries. In 1918, after the "Great War" (WWI) that resulted in the fall of both the Austrian-Hungarian Empire and the Ottoman Empire and the virtual redrawing of the map of Europe, the territory of my birth and childhood became the First Republic of Czechoslovakia. Today, the town that had been once the site of a few textile factories it is now a popular spot, as much for its boutiques as for its history. Even though I made my home in a faraway place as an adult, I carried with me the pride of having been a child of Mistek.

By the time I was born, the scars of World War I had largely faded, though vestiges of hunger and antagonism between Germans and Czechs remained. Buffered from the struggles of others far away, I was just another small boy in a small Eastern European town where the world's events had little effect on my activities. I was oblivious to political nuances unless they exploded in a schoolyard fight. Outside struggle was easy to ignore. Praha (Prague), the capitol, seemed to be on the other side of the globe.

And as for war, that could have been on the far side of the moon. For me, and for other children of the village, the world revolved around family and play.

For several years, when my mother and father were separated, I lived with my mother, Helena Botur, and her parents, Joseph and Josepha Pachta—my grandparents—in their small house on

3

Frydlanska Street in Mistek, along with my uncle on my mother's side, Victor. Our house was near a clear, flowing river, ideal for swimming and fishing. There were deer and small game in the forest. Our front garden overlooked the town's panorama with a large church in the background. We had a vegetable garden and pear, cherry, and apple trees. We raised hens, rabbits, and an occasional pig, but you would not call it a farm. Every home had a garden that supplied a good part of the family's needs. Since homes in our area did not have electricity in the 1920s and there was no refrigeration, cellars served as cold storage, or root cellars, for apples and potatoes and other provisions. I can recall helping often in the garden.

Within a half-hour's walk we would be in the small hills and forest, and within a few hours walk or by taking a train, there were the higher mountains—part of the Beskydy Mountains in Northern Moravia—of about four thousand feet, named Lysa and Radhost. These were the mountains that I skied on in the wintertime. There were no lifts, nor groomed slopes. A group of us would hiked up the steep mountain, which was covered in snow, for two or three hours with skis on our backs. Then we skied down in fifteen minutes. If there was enough light, we hiked back up for a second ski run. We were not short of energy and we often went to bed tired, but we were happy and had no idea that we could live any differently. It was an ideal young life in many ways, as we were sheltered from the turmoil that swirled around us. We were in a bubble, overindulged with innocence, unaware even that the adults in the 1920s and 1930s went to bed tired too, for different reasons. They were weary from difficult days and emotional struggles, and they didn't have time to play with us or to have hobbies—or be leisurely, like today. Only on Sundays did everyone attended church, some leisure, and family dinners together.

As for my immediate family, Mother was a delicate, sensitive woman with an insatiable romantic streak. Her long black hair framed a face that showed gentle determination. I remember her appearing so graceful to me. She was a concert violinist with the philharmonic orchestra before I was born, and she continued with her music after my birth. At times she played under the famous Czech composer and conductor Kubelik. She often traveled with the philharmonic, leaving me at home with her parents and Uncle Victor. When she was home, she practiced for hours on end. I watched the movements of the bow and her elegant fingers over the strings, creating the most wonderful sounds. Everything changed after she accepted my father back in 1932 and began spending more time caring for me and the household.

My father, Josef Botur, had left my mother when I was two years old. I was unaware of the reasons, but the fatherless household did not complicate my childhood. It was not at all strange for fathers to be off working somewhere. Many boys had fathers who were not at home, but divorces were uncommon. It was only as I grew older and overheard adults talking that I partially understood what had happened. He had gone to Poland to buy some cattle, but he did not return when his business was done. When he finally did return in the early 1930s, he continued working in the meatpacking business and a butcher shop in Ostrava, and he also opened his first American-style, fast-food shop, called ASO Inc., on the main street.

Life changed when he returned and we moved out of my grandparents' home. I missed the forest and fields and the hours spent playing or helping my uncle or grandparents—the memories that bathe my childhood in a golden light. Dates and times elude me after all these decades, but the picture of my mother playing the violin for endless hours is as fresh as if she had been playing this morning. She played to my children when she visited us in New York during the 1980s. I do recall visiting my father at work on some days and the women at his shop making a fuss over me, and he did too.

*Uncle Victor's vulcanization enterprise, being
the first in our area in the 1930s.*

I do not mean to dwell on my early childhood, but I wanted to
set the scene to show what gave me the strength to survive, to buck
up against one challenge after another and emerge stronger—more
tattered, maybe, but with fierce determination. And that means I
also have to introduce one other person who was important in my
early life, my Uncle Victor. Uncle Victor's various failed attempts
at making a living ranged from driving a taxi to vulcanizing tires
in our garage and, when that didn't work, using the same place
to manufacture ice cream. His mere presence added excitement
because he always had a story to tell, a banjo to play, and a love
of life. He was the high-spirited uncle who taught me to ice skate
by the time I was four. He had a skating rink on land rented from
the Sokol athletic organization. The sign above the rink was the
first thing I remember being taught to read: "In Healthy Body a
Healthy Mind." Funny that the motto would dominate my life, but
that is for later. Uncle Victor used a water hose to spray the field at

night, so as long the temperature stayed below freezing, we were able to skate.

Oh, yes, there is one more part of the family I want to introduce. Grandfather Josef made my boyhood one of delight. He looked after me when he was not working as a foreman at the textile mills. I will never forget that he gave me one of the best birthday presents I ever received as a child: it was a pocketknife. He showed me how to carve a small flute from a willow twig. The knife meant a lot to me because all of my young friends looked up to me once I had it. We did not have birthday parties like children do now, but Grandfather's gifts seemed to mark my growing up. One winter—I guess I was about four years old—I had stepped into his skis and tried to take a few steps with them. I did not get very far, but I made my point. The next birthday, Grandfather Josef presented me with my first skis. They were fashioned out of barrel staves and had leather strips for bindings, and he showed me how to use them. On another birthday, Grandfather brought home a dog for me, a wonderful German shepherd that followed me everywhere. In later years, we always had a German shepherd at our homes in the United States.

My grandmother Josefa Pachtova and Uncle Victor Pachta ran a small store out of a part of my grandparents' house, which also had a big yard where they raised chickens, pigs, and goats for home consumption. My grandma believed that drinking the goats' milk prevented tuberculosis, an infectious disease that was usually spread through contact with other kids at school. Penicilin was not invented yet. Our home was located on the main road to Koprivnice, the city where Tatra, the second-largest automobile manufacturer, after Skoda, was located. It was also home to textile mills and an iron works factory. My grandparents and uncle sold tobacco, food items, and miscellaneous merchandise, including textiles. Always trying to increase their business, my grandparents bought Uncle Victor a new franchise, Vulcanization, and built a garage onto the house to accommodate it. The process involved recycling old tires by heating the rubber to somehow make it into new tires. I used to love the smell of warm, fresh-smelling rubber, but not many shared my appreciation of the odor of rubber. Unfortunately, the effort was not a commercial success, so he dreamed of other paths—perhaps visiting his uncle Charles in Paris as he entertained at different clubs playing his new banjo. My grandparents were not happy with him when they discovered that the glass in a door to Grandmother's office was broken and crown notes, the Czech currency, were missing from her cash box. He was adventurous and I am sure he meant no ill, but he probably helped himself to some financing for his trip to Paris to visit Uncle Karel, or Charles as Uncle Charles preferred to be called.

Uncle Charles, who had a successful tailor shop catering to fashionable Parisian society, was probably not kindly disposed to the visit from his banjo-playing brother Victor. Years later in 1948, when I fled Czechoslovakia, I was desperately seeking help from Uncle Charles. He gave grudgingly and without any enthusiasm. To me, he appeared to be a very stuffy gentleman. He must have had our Great Grandfather Baron Pachta's genes. Uncle Victor probably hitchhiked much of his way to Paris, playing his banjo for dinner and places to stay on the way. I was happy to see him return to the store from Paris, and to the ice rink. The missing crown notes were forgiven somehow. Even if Uncle Charles had not offered a home or encouragement, I hoped Uncle Victor had a wonderful trip with his banjo, making his dream of playing in Paris a reality. I'd much rather experience the mischievous adventures of Uncle Victor than the dry success of Uncle Charles.

While we are on the subject of the not-very-likeable Uncle Charles, I might as well share a brief story of his family. He and his wife had two daughters and a son, Charles Jr., who became quite a successful concert pianist in Paris, where the family lived for as long as I can remember. I don't know what happened to the daughters, but Charles Jr. rebelled against his father and ran away with a woman to Argentina. In the Pachta family, such a thing was not acceptable, but Charles Jr. and his girlfriend eloped there, and he hoped to do well teaching piano. After a while, Charles Jr. became unhappy there, and the couple immigrated to the United States, ending up in New York. We reconnected, and for a few months, he taught my children piano. He and his wife were typical Bohemian artists; they thought the world owed them something. I tried my best to help him out, but it was not enough. After five years of living in the States, he decided to go back to Argentina because he thought that life in the States was too fast paced and people had to work too hard to make a decent living.

Grandmother's family lived near Vienna in a suburb called Neusiedel. Vienna was, after all, the cosmopolitan center of the Austrian-Hungarian Empire, and many Czechs gravitated to the area for the work it offered, just like my father had before he was married. My grandmother's maiden name was Feix, or Feixova for the woman. She once took me to Vienna to visit her relatives, but I have only a very faint memory of that event. The trip was special because we traveled such a long distance by train. When one is so young, one does not have interest in old people's conversations, thinking them boring and dull. I am convinced that it is only natural for us, as youths, to look ahead instead of paying attention to the moment if it does not directly affect us, and it's just as natural to regret it at an older age when we realize that we missed out on all those conversations that would have helped us understand more about our families and their pasts.

Unfortunately, by the time curiosity to know our families' pasts is piqued, the family members who could have shared stories are very few in numbers or have passed away, locking secrets away forever, unless we stumble upon some long-lost letter or memorabilia.

As boys, my friends and I had to invent our own toys or games, some of which were inspired by the hussars. After school, we often headed over to get as close as we could to the military barracks, or the so-called" Kasarny", which housed the mounted regiment. When they left the barracks and approached where we waited for a view of them, the sound of their horses' shoes on the cobblestones made an unmistakable beat. Out of nowhere they'd appear, regal in full-dress uniform—their red trousers with gold trim and sabers at their sides. The uniforms were a tradition dating back to the Austrian-Hungarian Empire. We boys all rushed to the road to wave to them and watched them passing upright in their saddles on their magnificently groomed horses.

They were gracious, allowing us to pat their horses and occasionally sharing their simple biscuits, or hard tack, with us. To us, having some of the hussars' hard tack—plain biscuits made of flour, water, and a dash of salt—was better than chocolate or a cookie. We looked at the mounted men wistfully, with a guileless envy, wishing to one day be one of them. It's amazing how vivid my memory is of the sight and sound of them, even the taste of hard tack, from a lifetime ago. For all the things that came naturally to me, schoolwork was not one of them. The truth is that I was never a good student. I always found lessons in things outside of school more interesting. Nevertheless, somehow, I managed. The teachers were mostly men, and there was no talking back to them. They were tyrants compared to today's teachers. During the German Protektorat, it was compulsory in schools to teach German, and during the Communist regime, it was Russian. Eighty years ago, if a teacher discovered that you had not done your homework or if you were bad, you had to go to the corner and kneel for fifteen minutes, sometimes with your arms held out as an extra punishment. I invite any young person to try this. Also, a wooden ruler was always handy to administer a good whack across your upturned palms. Punishment was administered swiftly for any misdemeanor, and there was no disputing authority. Detention after school was the most lenient consequence you could hope for.

On normal days, once the bell rang, signaling the end of the school day, we rushed out from the building, ran home, dropped our school bags in the corner of the hallway, grabbed a bite to eat from the kitchen, and rushed out again to meet friends in the fields. It was a daily routine of which we never tired. In winter, we finished our homework by the light of a petrol or kerosene lamp. Elementary school introduced me to discipline not only in academics and the classroom but also in sports. With discipline, I learned to start to concentrate and listen more to adults for answers than to my young friends.

Czech–German Emnity

I walked the twenty minutes to and from school every day, a route that crossed paths with German boys coming from their school. Occasionally, on the way home, my friends and I would get into skirmishes with them, each group vigorously hurling stones and expletives at the other with equal enthusiasm. I must confess that it was not always the German boys who instigated these skirmishes. Strange as it sounds now, it all seemed quite natural and ordinary then. Dislike between Czechs and Germans had been around for centuries, and our geographical coexistence was anything but peaceful. We learned to have a dislike for Germans at home from our parents, overhearing them speak of Germans as enemies. I am sure it was conversely the case for the German boys as well. None of us searched for any explanation for why these things were this way. We were young and unquestioning, and we perceived the scuffles as adventures. Occasionally, someone would get hurt, but we didn't complain because our parents would have disapproved.

Don Bosco Church

Outside of my grandfathers influenced, the biggest impact on my young life was made at Don Bosco, a modern Catholic church that also had recreational facilities for young people. The priests taught us how to paint and play table tennis and other games, including soccer, volleyball, chess, and billiards. However, all of this came along with a rule requiring us to attend mass on Sundays. Most of my memories from that period are very positive and the church had a big influence in the community on the behavior of young people. There was no real crime in our area, unless you consider pelting other kids with stones just because they were of a different ethnic background a crime.

Since my mother was a violinist, I was fated to take violin

lessons, followed by piano lessons when we moved to Ostrava. My mother was proud to be a violinist and always said, "Do not forget: you come from Pachtas ancestry, who have been great supporters of music." She proudly asserted that my great-great-grandfather was Baron Pachta, and my grandfather was descended from the baron's illegitimate son. The Pachta family lost its fortune to Hapsburgs in the revolutions of the seventeenth or eighteenth century. Mother explained how my great-grandfather, with the help of a priest, tried to receive some of the inheritance of the estate since my illegitimate great-grandfather was an heir and there were no legitimate heirs to his father, the baron. "Of course," she added, "no one had enough money to fight the Hapsburgs' claims on the property."

Another of Mother's stories told of Baron Pachta inviting Wolfgang Mozart to his palace in Prague. He did not let Mozart leave—practically held him hostage, until he composed festive music for an upcoming ball the baron had planned. She believed with all her heart that these stories were factual. I, too, now believe this could well be a true story since decades later, in the 1970s, I saw the incident described in a biography of Mozart.

When I was seven or eight years old, my mother enrolled me in the Little Lyons, a Boys Scout Club up to age ten in which they wore brown and blue outfits similar in nature to those of the Boy Scouts of America. Mother knew that learning independence and working with a team as a Little Lyon would be good for my development. Perhaps it would balance with the violin lessons that I was taking. As Little Lyons, my friends and I would go out in the woods and stay in tents overnight. We would sing around the fire in the evening, and we also had to learn how to clean the tents, set up our cots, and cook over an open fire. To become full-fledged Lions, we had to go on our own overnight trip in the forest. We stayed within earshot of adults and were given a whistle that we could blow if we thought that we were in danger. It was quite scary for us little boys. However, that was the only way we could be entitled to the special feather in our hats, the sign of full-fledged Little Lyon. Being scared and anxious at night was part of the adventure.

Depression of 1929

While I was learning how to survive in the woods, a much greater story of survival was unfolding. The Great Depression was closing in over industrialized nations, settling like fog and capturing in its unwanted mist millions of people, including my own parents. Only later in life did I begin to understand the struggle to put food on the table and a smile on a tired face. At seven years old, what did I know of starvation and hopelessness? My life was carefree, exuberant even. In 1929, I did not understand when Uncle Victor talked of a stock exchange crash in New York. As a little boy, I didn't have any idea that America even existed, but I remember that there were many hungry people in Czechoslovakia. People would try to get leftover coal for winter from the coal mines. On the way to the farmer's market, we would see clumps of them, small children among them, with jute sacks over their shoulders, walking determinedly the long way to the coal mines in Ostrava, where they discarded third-grade coal. I saw them picking the coal with their bare hands, filling their sacks to carry home. They could use these pieces of coal to warm themselves, or they would exchange it for some food. These were not nice memories from these hard times. It was through listening to Grandfather talking with Uncle Victor, or with his friends over a beer or cigar, that I started to learn more about these events. I was learning then to listen more to the adults around me.

It was a time of contrasts. Against the strain and struggle of an economic free fall, my mother decided that at age eight, it was time for me to start violin lessons with Mr. Tlusty, one of the older members of opera orchestra. I suspect that mother, in the recesses of her soul, hoped I would fall in love with music and become a professional musician.

At the same time, I learned the satisfaction of being rewarded for work. My father's brother, uncle Alfred, owned a restaurant, and it was up to me as a little boy to give out flyers in the summer at the open market. As a reward, Uncle Alfred would give me one frankfurter. It was my first real job and decades later, after the

Velvet Revolution, I told the story to a Czech who had lived under the Communist regimes for decades. He said that, at age eight, I was a born capitalist. I did not like the comment. I think it reflects all the conditioning lessons or brainwashing that the population went through in the communist era. Around that same time, or perhaps a year later, an incident happened which carved a memory that I have never been able to erase. I had a friend in school named Filipek, the Czech diminutive name for a young Philip. He came from a family of circus acrobats. One of their stunts was walking on the high wire or ropes without a safety net, he was a small star in their act. He was one of the few friends at that time whom I actually liked and admired. Occasionally he showed me a few tricks from his circus way of life. As circus entertainers, I assumed that they lived a hard life and had to struggle to earn enough to survive. He could not join in our games after school because he needed to rush home to practice walking the tight rope with his family. It required constant practice. However, he never complained. He was always in a good mood and smiling, and Mother liked him, often treating him to snacks. One morning, his bench at school remained empty. The teacher stepped into the classroom and announced that poor Filipek had fallen from a tightrope while practicing the prior afternoon. There were no safety nets. My young friend had been killed. We all attended his funeral, and with sadness we learned how fragile life can be, even for healthy young boys. The bench remained empty for the rest of the school year. We remembered him with sorrow every time we passed his empty bench and also prayed for his soul in Don Bosco. Suddenly, someone who was my size, my age, my friend was gone in a flash, forever. Life never felt as sure as it had again. That carefree camaraderie I had with my friends had been punctured.

Visit from Chicago, 1934

About two or three years later—it's not clear to me today, but it was before my grandmother died—we had visitors from Chicago, by name Knezeks. Grandfather looked up Chicago in our atlas for us and explained that the visitors were distant relatives from Grandmother's side. Their visit in the 1930s was about the single most exciting thing that happened in the village because they arrived with a driver in a Whippet automobile. The women had large hats and long dresses. The Knezeks family must have immigrated to the Chicago area in the middle of the eighteenth century, when so many Czechs did so that it was said that there were more Czechs in Chicago than in Prague in 1933 Chicago's mayor, Anton Cermak, who was later killed by an assassin's bullet meant for President Roosevelt, who was Czech-born from small town Kladno, and his parents had immigrated when he was a child. These distant relatives of mine had built a large, successful bakery I was told by my grandmother. A Knezeks daughter and her husband were the other couple in the car with them, touring Czechoslovakia in the chauffeured Whippet. They were visiting Grandmother on the way to Vienna, where her family came from. I watched how they tried to start the car by cranking it, and they allowed me to give it a try. The crank sprang back and hit my arm with a force that I can recall today. When they were leaving, the ladies handed me a big paper bill. It was to me an odd-looking piece of green and gray paper called a US dollar. I kept it for a long time with my other treasures in a cigar box that Grandmother had gotten me from the store. I do not remember what I did with the dollar except kept it as a souvenir. You certainly could not buy anything with it in Mistek, but, unbeknownst to me at the time, it was the first link I ever had to what would become my home.

The Whippet that fascinated me when the Knezeks visited was manufactured by the Willys-Overland Company, the company that later made the famous US Army jeeps of WWII, a detail that for some inexplicable reason made the experience with that particular car even more important in my mind.

Dreams of America, 1939–1940

My dreams of Whippets, Chicago, and America started slowly with the Knezeks' visit in the early 1930s but later began to take real shape after, of all things, seeing two movies. "*Snow White and the Seven Dwarfs*" was released by Disney in 1938 and it was a big hit in Moravia. Shortly afterward, Fred Astaire's "*Broadway Melody of 1939*" appeared, and I found myself tap dancing, Astaire style, and learning some English words. That movie made a big impression on me regarding what America would be like.

Navratilova's Coach George Parma at Tennisport

When I was twelve or fourteen, my school took the students on an outing by train to Uzhorod, an eastern part of Czechoslovakia that today is part of the Ukraine. While there, I bought a souvenir for my mother, a cigarette case, which cost a few cents at the time. The vase was left to me after my mother's death in 1996, and I still have it. Although it was inexpensive, to me it is one of my most precious antiques. Our class trip continued to the salt mines in Romania called Akna Slatina. For us, this was like going to the moon or being in a fairy tale, walking in the mines lit by acetylene lamps and seeing the walls full of crystals.

It was also at age fourteen that I had my first tennis lessons. It was 1936, and I was at Spa Luhacovice with my mother for two weeks. She decided that I was old enough, lanky enough, and probably on her nerves enough to dedicate some of that energy to a worthy endeavor like learning how to play tennis, which had always been one of her top interests after music. I did not realize it at the time, but my coach, Imre Houba, was a Davis Cup player. I enjoyed the first lesson and then took lessons every day for two weeks. When my mother and I got home, I continued to play at the Czechoslovak Lawn Tennis Club and the CLTK Club, which today is called Banik Ostrava. Ivan Lendl played at both clubs as child. During the Nazi occupation, when there was a shortage of food, my father's business helped pay for my tennis lessons. Since we were in the meatpacking business, I would pay for my tennis lessons with some salami or bacon instead of money because money was only paper that no one could eat. During and after the war, merchants and others preferred to exchange merchandise instead of paper money because of its limited value. I played as much tennis as I could, most of it with friends who were already far more advanced than I, but since we were friends and played other sports at the same time, they did not mind including me in all sports activities.

One day, our tennis professional, Mr. Ebel, announced that he had arranged for a match with a young player from another club to test my skills. He wanted to see how good I really was. I had been playing regularly for close to five years, and at nearly nineteen, I was not overly concerned when I heard that the young player who would be testing me was twelve.

"Hello," I said, greeting him while cheerfully walking onto the court. He nodded in return and held his wooden racquet up to signal that he was ready to hit. We warmed up slightly, and then the match started.

Kaboom! His serve overpowered me. I barely recovered in time to catch his forehand. How was I to know that a twelve-year-old named George Parma would become the best tennis player in Czechoslovakia in later years and the member of the Czech Davis Cup team. Because of illness, George had to stop playing for a few years. After recovering, he coached in the late 1950s

My hometown, where I started tennis lessons, called C.L.T.K.

Much later in my life, I would come to appreciate that, thanks to our parents and the role tennis played in our lives, fate put three

17

boys from the industrial town of Ostrava in New York, playing tennis and living in freedom in America. Mother had no way of knowing when she signed me up for two weeks of lessons where that experience would take me. I shall never know if she would have done something differently or chosen a different sport had she been able to see into the future. I do know that deep in her heart, she must have longed to see her son grow up to love music as she had. Fate, assisted by a happenstance decision to start me in tennis lessons as a way to develop social skills while she was summering at a spa, opened up a life that, after many detours, took me to the land I had dreamed about since distant relatives handed me a large bill and waved good-bye. Tennis had carried me to America, and I was happy to be along for the ride.

But long before 1952, when I set foot on the soil that would be home for the next sixty years of my life, an event occurred that would shape my life and affect everyone in our village.

Accident: August 16, 1936

Late in the evening of August 16, 1936, when I was a very young, unsophisticated fourteen-year-old, there was a loud banging at the door. Grandmother and Uncle Victor had gone to a farmer's market some fifty kilometers away to sell some textiles. Mother was performing in another city, and we did not expect her until the morning train. But the banging grew louder. Grandfather and I opened the door to find a policeman standing there next to his bicycle. Just seeing his serious face scared me. He told us that my grandmother and my uncle had been in a horrific truck accident about five kilometers from home, and both had been killed. The only phones then were at some railway stations or at the post office, so the policeman had come on his service bicycle.

Grandfather must have been in shock, but he pulled out his bicycle, hopped on, and put me on the front frame, and we rode out into the darkness. The policeman had told us where to go. He explained that, on the way home, the truck's brakes had failed. When we arrived, we looked on in shock and horror when we saw how the truck had gone across the bridge, crashed through the railing, and plunged twenty meters (the height of a four- or five-story building) down into a ravine. Grandmother, Uncle Victor, the driver, and nine others from our village were in the truck. No one survived. About a hundred meters from the bridge was a house where the police had laid out the eleven twisted, mangled bodies along the front wall to form the most horrible scene that I have ever, to this day, witnessed.

There were petrol or kerosene lanterns illuminating the dead bodies so that family members could identify them. Two of their heads were so broken that I could see their brains. Splinters of bones pushed out from their limbs. It was an appalling sight of horror in that silent night, illuminated by the ghastly flickering of the petrol lanterns. For some reason, I was the one trying to calm my grandfather, as far as I can remember.

I do not know how we managed to get back home, but it must have been by the same bicycle that we had come on. I don't recall whether Grandfather wept or whether I did. I don't recall how we slept, if we did at all. I only remember the arrival of my mother the morning after, back from the concert, and how she sent me off immediately on the train to Ostrava to inform her sister about the deaths of her mother and brother Victor. It was my first trip without a parental escort on the train. It was a great experience since I had never before paid attention to how to buy the tickets or how many stops there would be before Ostrava, my destination. I don't recall how she reacted or if she came back to Mistek with me. I cannot recall the funeral. I don't recall much of the weeks and months after the tragedy. When the truck plunged down the ravine, my life as I had known it crashed with it. The next months were a blur, the harmonious household shattered.

Grandfather had lost his wife and his son, the uncle who had patiently taught me how to ice skate and shared the joy of it with me. Our family, so stable in the home of my mother's parents, had dwindled and shriveled in a single moment on a single night. Now we would sadly share a house half emptied. There are things you never forget as long as you live, and the sights of that night are ones I will never forget.

Life in Ostrava, 1932–1948

It was at the end of 1937, when things started to really change in our household. After several years of separation, my mother accepted my father back, and we moved from my grandfather's house to a nice apartment house at Stodolni Street 31 in Ostrava. Father was well established in the meatpacking business. In addition, he had a small fast-food store, called ASO, on the main street of Ostrava. It was considered American style at the time, and it was successful. He also had a wholesale cattle business. We lived across from the slaughterhouse and the municipal cattle market. Almost daily, a train with at least a hundred cattle arrived at the municipal market to be distributed to smaller firms and slaughtered. Father would just walk across the street to his office, where he employed two accountants and a secretary.

I continued going to school in Ostrava and made many new friends. There were many coffee shops where young people met. At one point, I met my first love, Vlasta Hofmanova, in her father's bakery and coffee shop. Our affair lasted a few years. When I left to study at Charles University in Prague, she married a nice, attractive, young businessman named Vavrecka and soon had children. I was very happy for her, and we remained friends.

View of part of Ostrava, with Coal mines and Steel mills in background.

My mother gave her my address in New York, and about

twenty-five years after we had met, after her husband died, she visited New York and stayed a few days in our house in Long Island. She asked me to help her to sell one of her valuable paintings at Sothebys which I did auction for her. She told us that her son was working as an engineer in Iran, and a few years later I met him in Frankfurt when he moved from a job in Teheran. Since then, however, I have lost contact.

Ostrava is an industrial town, mostly coal mining and steel manufacturing. Not far away were the large steel mills. As a boy, I visited them at times, fascinated by the images of the hot steel pouring out of the ovens and then being formed into ingots. Often, in the evenings, I saw coal miners emerge from the mines with lantern their faces caked with coal dust. I remember some occasions when a few of them did not come back at all. The coal mines were not operated at high safety or even acceptable standards, so accidents happened often, and accidents in coal mines are often tragic. When I wasn't there, I spent every free moment with friends playing table tennis, soccer, or chess or dating.

After the war, Father started, an additional business venture. It was a large pig farm, with land he leased from a farmer named Pravda. He copied the American system of mechanically feeding the pigs, and they gained weight quickly. Pig farming was not an easy business; many pigs succumbed to sicknesses, and perhaps 10 percent died from diseases. During the war, there were shortages of food so, we boiled the diseased carcasses at high temperatures to make them suitable to eat. Today, far lesser strains of disease are carefully monitored and fear of the swine flu has altered the exportation and importation of pigs from the UK and Europe. But in those days, the availability of once-diseased and then freshly boiled meat, which we gave to our friends and employees, was valuable. They had food and were able to save precious rationing coupons for other items. Nobody complained or got sick. Some even traded the meat for cigarettes or coffee and then turned around and traded those items for others in the constantly busy black market.

Being the son of a butcher taught me some unusual lessons. I pleased my father once by creating a food supply for our pig farm. I bought about twenty milk canisters, and I gave a few crowns to my friends. They went around to restaurants collecting leftovers, which I loaded onto an old army truck that we had an opportunity to buy from the UNRA supply, and we hauled them to the pig farm. We combined the leftovers with rotten or frozen potatoes and cooked the slop in kettles. The chefs in the restaurants received one pig a year for the leftovers they contributed. "You have done well, my son," my father said to me in a rare moment of praise, words I would treasure.

Not all of my ideas were so good, though. One evening, I had the opportunity to go to a students' ball in town, and I needed a black tie suit. I managed to exchange food coupons for one black tie from a tailor. I looked so good. I was pleased with my black tie because I wanted to impress some of the girls. My father told me to be home early since we had work to do in the morning. After some bargaining, he gave me a curfew of one o'clock. Of course, the party was great and I made my way home afterward, sneaking in very quietly at three o'clock. Just as I was starting to undress, I heard my father's voice: "Stay as you are, and do not change." he said. "We are leaving for work at four thirty to feed the pigs. I told you to come at one o'clock." Just imagine—after a party night with too much wine, you have to work a shift of preparing leftovers for the pigs. Most people never see the way the pigs' food used to be prepared or smell the rancid odor that fills your nostrils so you can hardly breathe. Pig feed back then consisted of old smelly meats, potatoes that had frozen and spoiled, intestines from the slaughterhouses, and leftovers from the restaurants, all cooking in huge kettles. Just the smell was enough to make me sick. As an extra punishment, I had to work in my black tie suit. You should have seen me after just half an hour!

My mother did not have it any easier than I did; my father enforced discipline like an old-time Austro-Hungarian monarch. In his house, the man was the boss, and everything he said had to be done. He was demanding and very rarely hugged my mother or me. He was a big drinker, smoker, and gambler but also a good provider. In his heart, he was a good person. He helped many people, as I have heard over the years. In his business, there was plenty of time during the evenings, so he went to a smoky beer hall to play cards with his buddies. My mother refused to go with him, so she would send me off at nine or ten o'clock at night in the summer to bring him home. Since my father would not listen, I had to sit with him for hours while he and his friends finished the game.

"Father, let's go home. Let's go home," I would plead. But if he was losing, I did not dare say anything. I never will forget one evening when he came home late and in a bad mood. The food was already cold, and he complained to my mother about it. In his anger, he threw the plate through the window. Occasionally, he could have a very violent temper with us or his employees, but basically he was a good man. However, what he said was a law. In the 1930s and '40s, in the Eastern European countries, men were macho and had to show their dominance in front of their buddies.

Once, during one of my mother's vacations to Spa Luhacovice, I found my father in our apartment with another woman in a compromising position. I was shocked and ran out the door. Later, he tried to explain that sometimes men have certain desires. He took me out for a beer and to a house for loose women. I was embarrassed and couldn't wait to finish the beer and get out. Suddenly, I was growing fast and becoming aware of life around me and learning about business, friendships, sex, and love. It was difficult to figure out right from wrong in business and friendship, and the difference between sex and love were even less clear.

Father's Friend Hafran, 1937

Some of my father's friends were already aware of a growing dangerous political situation with the Germans. A Friend of my father's, Leopold Hafran, came to visit us around 1937. He asked my father for financial help to leave for Argentina. He was Jewish and was concerned for his future in our country. I was too young to understand their discussion, which sounded mysterious and exotic to me. When I asked Father what it was all about, he just shrugged his shoulders and said, "You would not understand." Years later, my mother received a few letters from Hafran telling us of his life in Argentina, where he had opened a biscuit factory. Unfortunately, I was so busy with my life then that I lost touch.

In Ostrava, my mother enrolled me in piano lessons with Mrs. Sramkova, but after some years, that ended without much success, just as the earlier violin lessons had. While the lessons were less than memorable, they led to an acquaintance that, in turn, led to a lifelong friendship. Mrs. Sramkova had a daughter, who was nicknamed Muki who grew up to be a beautiful young lady, talented and hard working. At sixteen, she became a junior European champion in ice figure skating and went on to participate in the Olympics. During a brief easing of political restrictions, Muki was able to leave Czechoslovakia in 1968 to enter into a contract with the famous skating show Holiday on Ice. There she met up with another famous Czech figure skater, Aja Vrzanova, who was the first woman to do the double Lutz and was a two-time world champion, and an Olympic Gold Medal winner. Both women settled in New York, and we all became friends. If I had not had piano lessons, I might never have known these two amazing women whose parallel stories revealed so much about the world of sports achievement in the free world.

My best friend since high school was Leon Fiza, a very bright student. We sat next to each other in class, and he often helped me when I had been lazy or was otherwise just not prepared, allowing me to look over his shoulder at his paper work. When I left Czechoslovakia in 1948 as a refugee, he was one of the few people who corresponded with me regularly while I was in Australia and in the States. I have all of his letters, and in many of them, there are black areas—words that were censored by the Communist regime. The letters were very sad. One could compile a book on the lives and sufferings of intellectuals living under communism. During Fiza's older years, party officials refused to give him a job suitable for his education because he would not join the Communist party.

Instead, the only work they gave him involved manual labor, including grave digging. He explained in those letters how difficult life was for him, his wife, and his children. I am sorry that he did not live long enough to see democracy rise again.

An opposite example is a friend with whom I used to play tennis and whose father was already a bigwig in the Communist party when we met. He got a job as a soccer coach overseas, and as a party member he enjoyed many privileges. Many other people my parents knew joined the Communist party despite not being party believers—they joined out of necessity to feed their families.

Fathers' Psychological Method

By the time I got to high school, we had moved to Ostrava, but due to overcrowding, they sent nine of us boys to a school in Cesky Tesin, a town at the Polish border that was approximately fifty kilometers from Ostrava. We lived in a boarding house and would walk to school from there. The other boys influenced me, or I influenced them. We preferred the lessons of woods and streams to those of the classrooms, perfect for rainy days was the nearby pub's billiards room in the back, where we spent more happy hours than any of us would have admitted.

One rainy day, the door to the billiards room flung open, and I was shocked to see my father and his driver filling the doorway. My father took off his leather coat, held it out for his driver to take, and motioned for me to go to the billiards table. He had received a report from the school showing an unusually high number of sick days for his healthy son, and doubting that his healthy son had suddenly become a sickly student, he wasted no time in diagnosing the illness himself and perhaps offering a cure. I don't know if the landlady at the boarding house or someone at the school told him where we were or if he just used his instincts, but he came prepared with a stiff leather strap which was used to herd cattle. He took the strap and pulled me over the billiard table and beat me. The four other boys were shocked and wisely remained silent, but foolishly they remained until it was too late. Father was not yet done. He grabbed the two nearest boys and administered his beating as a favor to their fathers. The other two saw the lesson in store for them and jumped through the window of the billiards room. That evening, the landlady at the boarding house applied some iodine to our cuts. For the rest of our high school days in Cesky Tesin, none of us five boys had another sick day.

Grandfather's Death

When we moved to Ostrava, Grandfather stayed behind in the house in Mistek. I never knew the explanation, whether it was my father's or my grandfather's wish that he stay in his family home rather than move to an apartment in a far larger city. Mother and I would go back to visit Mistek as often as possible. While it was easy for me, as a child, to adapt, our moving must have been one more heartbreak for Grandfather. First, in August of 1936, he lost his wife and a son, and less than three years later, he lost his son Ferdinand. Our move to Ostrava left him completely alone in the house. The home that was so full of life a short time before now held only memories and emptiness, and I missed my grandpa. It is not surprising to me that healthy old Grandfather died within a year. He probably died of a broken heart.

The house still stands. Never shall I forget that August night in 1936. Now, when I visit, I leave flowers at the bridge, the bridge I often think took my youth.

Grandmother and Grandfather

My Father and Mother

Mother's Grandmother, her sister and brother, from Vienna

Chapter Two:
Escape

Entered Charles University, 1945

Father decided how I spent my school vacation time, and there was no arguing with what he said. Two thirds of that time was spent working with him, either in the factory learning to make sausages or at the slaughterhouse. Some vacations he send me to work in some of his friends workshops to experience hardship. Occasionally, I went with him to buy cattle in the countryside, where I learned that a handshake was as solid as a binding, written contract. By the time I was sixteen, my father's friends in the meatpacking house pronounced that I was ready to be initiated as a full-fledged butcher. To prove it, I had to kill a calf, skin it, and cut it into parts, and then I was supposed to complete the ritual by drinking a small cup of the calf's blood. In this way, I was acknowledged as a Tovarys—a worker, colleague, comrade. It was an unofficial sort of graduation into butchery but one that meant a good deal inside the packing house. After that, if a person continued in that profession, he would be called a master butcher. I never became a master. My father—who was still dominating my life—determined that I would be a lawyer, I enrolled in Charles University in Prague in 1945. None of us had a crystal ball so how would we know that the war that raged around us would explode on campus, closing the doors of what was then the leading university in Czechoslovakia.

For three years, following a demonstration between the two sectors—German and Czechoslovakian, fighting bitterly and openly over official language, insignia, and, ultimately, control—the university closed for three years. Nine students died in the demonstrations, and another hundred were rounded up and sent to a prison camp, where more than two dozen perished. The university didn't reopen until 1945. The day of its closure, November 17, is today marked as International Students Day around the world.

Until the Nazi occupation, I knew little about politics. When I picked up a newspaper, it was the sports section I read. But a child or even a young man can become an accidental student, overhearing conversation despite not listening intently. What I heard my father and his friends saying about politics and the possibility of another war subconsciously influenced my thinking. It was around this time that many of the Germans in our town started to protest against the government of Czechoslovakia. They lived in the Sudetenland, border areas of Czechoslovakia adjoining Germany. Many of the Sudeten Germans wanted to see the Sudeten annexed to Germany. Konrad Henlein, the leader of the Nazi German Party in Czechoslovakia, visited Hitler and returned with a promise that, since the Sudeten were German-speaking areas, they would be annexed by Germany in the event that they occupied us. It has been written about extensively in the many histories of this prewar period.

Chamberlain and Peace Forever, 1938

I had started to pay more attention to political events, reading more than just the sports in the newspapers and trying to understand what all of this meant. France and England had promised to help defend our republic against the Germans in case of a war. Then they met with Hitler and sacrificed us. They thought that by signing a treaty turning the Sudetenland over to Germany, peace would last forever. I remember the headlines in the newspaper with a picture of Chamberlain at the London airport holding a piece of paper above his head that read "Peace for our

Time." This was the ill-conceived Munich Agreement of September 1938, later referred to as the Munich Betrayal. Czechoslovakia was not invited to participate in the negotiations but waited outside. They were told afterward to turn over the Sudetenland. Six months later, in March 1939, the balance of Bohemia and Moravia were occupied by German forces, and Slovakia became a puppet state. I remember that my father was disappointed by French Prime Minister Daladier and British Prime Minister Chamberlain, who sold us to Hitler. I also remember the night very well when the Germans arrived in tanks and motorized vehicles.

My mother and I were that evening at the opera to see Dvorak's *Rusalka*. Halfway through the opera, everything stopped abruptly. The director walked onstage, and a hush fell over the audience as he dramatically announced, "The German troops just entered our town. They have occupied us." Everyone in the theatre got up and, in a unified voice, sang the Czech national anthem and left the Opera and many cried. It was a very sad and depressing moment. The occupation happened without any resistance, since the negotiations in Munich about peace were on the way, the Czech army did not have any directions for the resistance. The only place where a few bullets were exchanged were in Mistek, a small town where I grew up.

PS: When living in the Bahamas later in life, a friend of ours read my book (Christina Hunter, Chairman of Fundraising for the Metropolitan Opera) and was really impressed by the story of the opera Rusalka being stopped because the German army just occupied us. In my honor she requested to have the opera broadcasted by MetLife Broadcast at the Lyford Cay Club.

Life in the German Protectorate of Bohemia and Moravia under Nazis

Things started to change in our lives quickly. The Germans staffed government offices with their own people, the Sudeten

Germans. They installed a new Czech president, Emil Hacha, as a puppet president. The newspapers described Hitler's humiliation of the elderly, would-be negotiator Hacha making him wait eight hours after long trip by train from Prag before receiving him. Hacha tried to get concessions from Hitler for our occupied country, but he had nothing to bring to the table and Hitler seized on the old man's lack of power. While he was waiting, the German troops were already crossing our borders. We were at their mercy. The Germans sent us and other eastern countries' people as laborers to German factories that were later bombed almost daily by the Allies. Many of our people were killed there. The only thing we did not have to do was join the German army, except as volunteers. I cannot remember that any of the people ever volunteered. Swastikas hung in all the government offices. Any time someone entered their offices to ask for anything, he had to lift up his right hand, If he did not, he was refused service and could get into serious trouble. Fear ruled. *Victimization* was the operative word. Germans started to ration our food with coupons for everything. Each family received an allotment of coupons based on the number of adults and children in the household. Ration coupons became a form of currency, and trading became the new way of life. The black market was essential. We could not survive without it, as most of the produce that was grown in Czechoslovakia was sent to Germany. Hitler's rapidly expanding army soon occupied Poland, Yugoslavia, France, and Russia, as well as a good part of North Africa. Several of our Jewish friends had foresight to leave to England or other western countries.

During the war, my friend Hoffman, whose sister I was dating at the time, got involved in delivering messages to the Yugoslav partisans. Some of the goals were to inform about the movements of the German troops and the train routes for supplies of munitions. I was his partner and accompanied him on one of these trips. Our documents were checked at almost every train station. Although I was less informed than my friend, I was, as I look back on it, incredibly lucky, always managing to get the right papers to travel with bribery using food supplies. That was my contribution to help my friend arrive safely at the destination. Still, I was constantly terrified of being arrested. We went by train from Ostrava to Brno, Vienna, Graz, and the final destination, Klagenfurt, which was on the border of Yugoslavia. Hoffman delivered coded messages to a food store in town. It was an eventful trip. The train stopped between Vienna and Graz because of air raids (*anflugs*) by American B-12 bombers. The train would stay idle for an hour, and we would run out from the train when there was an alarm, only returning after the all-clear signal. The personnel on the train would conduct several inspections of passengers' documents. Because of the *anflugs*, we had to stay overnight in Graz in a small place where people had just finished producing what we thought was apple juice. After drinking about two glasses, we found out that it was as much as 50 percent alcohol because it was made from apples that had been left to ferment.

The balance shifted after the famous battle for Stalingrad. We could see the beaten and exhausted Germans moving to the western front to help fight the Allied invasion of Normandy. We knew from the German news that the Russian army under Marshal Konev was one of the most brutal units. It was rumored to have dismembered bodies and tortured the Germans and their sympathizers, especially in the Ukraine. The torture method of waterboarding used in Guantanamo Bay seems miniscule compared to the methods that the Russians used against the Germans so were the same methods used by Germans. The Ukrainians hated the Russians then, and many fought alongside the Germans. Even today there are substantial political differences between the Ukraine and Russia. We heard horrible stories during that time. Later, I witnessed some on my own as the Russians replaced the Germans as our occupiers, committing their own atrocities, as I describe later in Krutsky's story. It's said that Stalin appreciated Marshal Konev for his ruthlessness. Marshal Konev went on in 1956 to command the crushing of the Hungarian Uprising. Western powers could only watch on the news. Tension between Russia and the United States increased tremendously during this time.

The German Protectorate became the democratic Czech

Republic out of necessity to survive under the Nazi regime from 1938 to 1945. During the war, though many Czechs were sent to concentration camps. Atrocities occurred like the one at Lidice, where the Nazis executed about two thousand Czechs as revenge for Reinhard Heydrich's assassination. Many books have been written about these murders, and the events surrounding them will be in Czech history forever.

The country continued to survive until the Communist regime took full control in 1948 but the Russians kept most of their army and moved only some divisions out of the Czech Republic. The Communists took over the government and jailed or sent to Siberia whoever was against them. They nationalized not only all industries but also small businesses, like my father's. During the German occupation, in the "Protectorate," people were able to keep their small businesses, but the biggest percentage of whatever they produced in manufacturing or from farming went to the Germans. During communism even in their own businesses, people became employees of the state.

No matter how hard people worked or tried to build a life, they were always aware of the political forces that swirled around them, threatening them. There was a palpable awareness of vulnerability, a keen sense that nothing was necessarily permanent, and in a bizarre way, it may have made them stronger, preparing them to adapt. Having seen a country going through constant changes, I developed a sense of adapting early on. I started as an eight-year-old boy when I handed out leaflets to earn money for hot dogs. Like everyone else, my family was constantly under pressure to survive the political change.

The Marshall Plan, which helped all of Western Europe get back on its feet economically, created huge change. We had been receiving packages from the United Nations Relief Aid (UNRA) with canned food and goods. Whatever we found in the food packages labeled "UNRA" usually contained delicious food. For my father's business, we received a small, three-quarter ton GM army truck for a minimal price from UNRA. That way, the army vehicles did not need to be shipped back to the United

States and were made useful in the reconstruction of Europe. The small truck was a big help for our business. It was exciting for me to drive this vehicle knowing that it must have been driven through the battlefields of Europe. However, due to the political fighting between the East and West, Moscow would not allow Czechoslovakia to join in the Marshall Plan, so we were lucky to have gotten at least a truck before Marshall Plan help was refused.

"Hallo? Hallo? … Ici Radio Toulouse, vouz avez entender a la langue de Czech."

During the Nazi regime Germans had a great advantage in controlling what we could listen to. We really had to fish hard on a crystal radio set for the stations we wanted to hear, those not blocked by Germans. Remember, it was not long before that many of the homes had gotten electricity. They used petrol lamps in the evening and a coal or wood stove for heating. How can you explain such things to your children today? We had gotten electricity in 1928 along with the first radio. Later, in the 1940s, during the Nazi occupation, we were lucky if we heard some news from the West BBC radio or the Canadian Broadcasting Company, via London. We had to listen in secret because independent news about the war was forbidden. What we heard, we passed on to neighbors we trusted, just as they did for us. We called it our bush telegraph. We relied on neighbors' whispering to one another as soon as the broadcasts came on. At that time, CBC was inviting migrants to Canada, even paying for travel expenses. Many times, I thought that if there were an opportunity to leave, I would take it. I had no idea that fate was going to do it for me. France was occupied by Germans, with economic and dictatorship conditions similar to those in the Czech Protectorate. However, that part of France was run under Marshal Petain during that time, with its capitol in Vichy. Finding news was difficult because broadcasters had to move their mobile stations daily to evade capture by the Germans, but the "bush telegraph" worked, with neighbors keeping neighbors informed about how the war was progressing.

Building a Bunker in the Cellar

For all his harsh ways, my father was a man of action. War and its injustices, small and large, ate away at his conscience like it ate away at our innocence. Inspiration drove him. After hearing horrible war stories, he gathered a few friends, and together they built a bunker in the cellar of our four-story apartment house. It had accommodations to sleep about ten people in four bunk beds and rations for a week.

Russian tanks plowed through the town of Ostrava. We held our breath, scared to move, as the tanks rumbled through the town, every rotation of every wheel brought them closer. Behind the heavy trucks walked Marshal Konev's infantry. There was still some resistance from German snipers from the roofs or windows, but the Russian soldiers were tired and didn't react if some of their comrades were killed. They just kept going. For the next few days, we stayed in the bunker. Russian tanks moved through town with the rest of the motorized army following, along with the infantry on the vehicles or marching through. In the meantime, the occupying forces took to looting. They raped women in many cases; some of those women never recovered, and their lives were haunted by the memories that became daily nightmares. The few German soldiers hid in the forest, and the German resistance and the newspapers called them werewolves. Most of them were eliminated by the Russians within a few months.

"Krutsky! Come Out, You German Swine!"

On the day that Russian tanks moved through our town, they never gave the Germans time to blow up the bridge over the river to the north of Ostrava. By late afternoon, the shooting slowed. It was quiet in the bunker at first and then totally silent. "Father, can we go up?" I whispered to my father, hoping for fresh air. My father used no words to answer me. His glare was enough warning. He was firm in his decision that we would stay at least one more night in the bunker. Late in the evening, two Russian soldiers suddenly appeared outside the house with machine guns accompanied by one Czech civilian wearing a red armband displaying a hammer and sickle. I discovered later that many of the members of the Communist party who were underground during the war years had begun declaring themselves commissars.

During the Nazi occupation, we sympathized with our Russian brothers. But then they claimed that the power of the provisional, lawless Communist government was in their hands. So the Czech commissar shouted into the bunker, "Krutsky! Come out, you German swine! Or we are going to throw a grenade in your bunker."

Krutsky was a German businessman who had lost an arm long before the war. He and his family lived in the same apartment building as we and our other neighbors, the Starostas, Weiners, and Pasternaks. With just one arm, he could not be a soldier, so he was in charge of manufacturing shoes for the German army. His wife and son heard the commissar call out his name, and they started to cry. The rest of us said he was not going to come out. We knew what could happen. The Russian soldiers had been shooting civilians without any reason other than that they were Germans or collaborators. Then, when the commissar again threatened that he would throw a grenade into our bunker if Krutsky did not come out, it fell to me to try to reason with him since I was the only one who could speak and understand a bit of Russian. The situation in the bunker was tense; some of our tenants tried to calmly persuade Krutsky to go out, naively thinking that nothing would happen to him. I remember his wife clutching their little son and crying. The threat of a hand grenade was still on everybody's mind and the situation was bordering on hopeless. I raised my voice, in spite of my father's objection, and I shouted out in Russian that he was not an SS man, that we were Czechoslovakian and Slavic brothers and Stalin would not approve, killing their Slavic brothers. It was late in the evening and we could hear the Czech commissar, who spoke perfect Russian, say, "He is your prisoner." Then he left to continue his murderous activities elsewhere. I tried to reason with the two remaining Russian soldiers. "Krutsky is not an SS," I said in the best Russian I knew. "With one arm," I pleaded, "how can this man be a soldier?"

Krutsky's wife was screaming holding her son in her arms, pleading for him not to leave the safety of the bunker. He was afraid to step outside but knew that if he didn't, we could all perish. His only crime had been to follow orders to use his one good arm to make shoes for the German army. Seconds felt like minutes, minutes like hours. I said, "I will go with him outside. They will not harm me since they heard me pleading for mercy in Russian and Czech. Mother and Father were in disbelief and urged me not to go. I didn't expect any danger to come from accompanying Krutsky outside, and I was trying to be helpful to him by translating his conversation with the Russian soldiers. After all, they were Slavic brothers, and at the age of twenty-two, I felt in my heart some responsibility to help an innocent neighbor. I had very often heard in the Russian news broadcasts an idiom saying, "Stalin skazal," which meant "Stalin's orders." I had used that idiom every time I had had a conversation with the soldiers, and it had worked. They respected it, and I planned to use it again as we stepped outside. The Czech commissar left and the soldiers were more at ease. We were in the front yard and in Russian hands. The soldiers ordered Krutsky and me to follow them to a room in the small building across the street where tired and drunk Russian soldiers were sleeping on the floor of a building. Some of them were so drunk that they were unconscious; I found out later that they had been mixing alcohol with benzene or ethyl alcohol. We heard that some of them became blind from drinking it.

Inside the building poor Krutsky got on his knees, raised his only arm, and cried out, begging for mercy. I had never witnessed a grown man so helpless, desperate, pleading, begging, crying, knowing that his life could end in a second. Did his life flash before him? Whatever went through his mind or the terror caused a phenomenon I have never seen before or since. I watched in disbelief as in a split second, his entire head of hair turned white. Years later at my Tennis Club, I asked a psychiatrist member if that had been my imagination, but he said it could happen to people under extreme stress. The white hair apparently shocked or impressed the Russian soldiers. One of them took Mr. Krutsky by the neck and threw him out of the door, saying, "*Ty nemuz. Ty si. Baba!*" roughly translated, he had said, "You are not a man! You are an old crying woman!" The door was half glass and shattered when they hurled his body against it, sending glass shards and splinters flying. Mr. Krutsky ran and ran. I also have to mention that, with no disrespect intended for these young, drafted solders, they were very primitive people from the rural areas of Siberia or Mongolia. They did not know what toilets were. They thought they were something to wash or drink in. I had to feel sorry for their almost inhuman condition: hungry, dirty, tired, full of lice, and pushed on unmercifully by the officers or commissars. Regardless, we never found out what happened to Mr. Krutsky.

After the Russians let Mr. Krutsky go, I tried talking with them. They wanted to know how we lived. My father came looking for me and said he knew how to keep such rough soldiers happy.

He brought two bottles of Slivovitz that he had hidden along with some lard in the cellar in case of an emergency. We drank to Slavic brotherhood, and even I had to have a shot of Slivovitz with them. We did not want them to think that we did not like them. That would not be good. Father and I both left at dawn, relieved that we had saved Krutsky and made a few Russian soldiers happy with drinking to new Slavic brotherhood. We had no idea what would happen next.

Rape

The next morning, the Russians discovered that Krutsky had a good-looking wife because she searched for him the next day, asking everyone his whereabouts. But no one knew where he was. Was he in hiding? Had he fled? Where? She was frantic, begging for someone to answer. The next day, when everyone left the bunkers and returned to their homes, one of our neighbors discovered that many Russian soldiers had brutally raped Mrs. Krutsky. I found out later by overhearing my mother telling our neighbor that she was so cut up inside that she barely survived. Every Czech family hid their daughters in the cellars or in the woods. The raping of women and girls and the plundering of houses and shops had started, as had the personal demands for anything of worth that an individual had. As we walked on the street, the Russians would come up and say, *"Davaj casy,"* meaning "Give me your watch," and we did. What choice did we have faced with the gun?

Our NKVD Guest

The Russian command placed officers and soldiers with families throughout the city. They all drank a great deal. Shortly after the disappearance of the one-armed Mr. Krutsky and the horrific rape of his wife, a Russian major with several medals on his uniform was assigned to move from NKVD headquarters into our apartment. He was a major in the Russian army who seemed to be well educated and very pleasant, and one evening when he had a few drinks with my father, he loosened up and started to tell us a little bit about the way of life in Russia. He was completely baffled as to why we would want communism in our country. My father spoke to him often, but I did not know what it was all about. Maybe he thought I was still too young to be involved. The major was reassigned and transferred a few months later, and I have always regretted not learning more during his presence.

Fighting a War and Killed on Motorcycle

My father frequented a bar and restaurant on the corner near the house prior to 1938. The Jewish family who owned the restaurant was named Fishl. Before the Germans occupied our town, the Fishls were able to move to Russia. I'm not sure, but I think that my father, who kept much to himself, may have helped them leave. In the second or third week of our so-called Russian liberation in Ostrava, the Fishl son came to visit us. Years had passed since we had last seen him, and we were stunned to see him outfitted in the highly decorated uniform of a Russian captain. Among his medals was the highest of Stalin's Order. It was a strange calling card for a visit to the place where he had spent most of his childhood and where his parents had lived. We had not yet felt the brunt of communism, and we looked at Captain Fishl remembering the teenager who had spent many an evening pummeling the punching bag in our yard, practicing to become a lightweight boxing champion.

He explained that he had received Stalin's High Order as the commander of the tank unit that broke through the German lines in the Ukraine and again in the south Carpathian Mountains, a tragic blood bath in 1944 known as the Battle of Dukla Pass, which had thousands of casualties. He had drinks at our house and said he had to return to his unit in two days. I tried to imagine what it would be like to be in his place, living through the barrage of cannon fire and thousands of bullets, and then returning to a homecoming in the town of your childhood. He visited a few bars with his Russians comrades. Following morning, he was due to return to his unit. A few days later, we heard that he had been driving a motorcycle when he hit a tree and was killed instantly. What a sad story. I am sure many similar stories were shared before and after the war when soldiers got drunk.

Slavic Brotherhood vs. Common Enemy

Since we were a Slavic nation, the Russians called us brothers, and at the beginning we welcomed them with open arms. Radio propaganda encouraged the brotherhood that for us felt natural. We believed the Russians were our liberators. We shared a common enemy, Germany. Our common hatred for and distrust of anything German was so great that it lulled us Czechs and probably many Slavics into a naive trust of Russia. It was a hard lesson, but we began to understand its consequences over the next two years as our country was controlled by the NKVD (later the KGB) and our view of our Slavic brothers started to metamorphose. They committed the same atrocities as the Nazi Gestapo. People were jailed, tortured, and sent to labor camps. There was no possibility that democracy could be restored in our country under those circumstances.

Communist cells had become entrenched everywhere—in schools, labor unions, worker organizations, and entertainment. They especially watched Czech intellectuals and the communist cells denounced anyone speaking against the Soviet regime. Brother denounced brother, and nobody trusted anyone anymore. During the first few weeks of chaos in May of 1945, people disappeared, never to be heard from again. The rumors were that the Russians sent thousands to Siberia. Just like the Germans had Nazi swastikas on their arms, the new regime wore armbands, but now they were red, with hammer and sickle, and worn by Czech Communist commissars who were directed by the Soviets.

From 1945 to 1948, the Czech Republic still had some independence. Under President Benes, it was nominally democratic before the communists took control in February 1948, which they did with the help of social democrats, who gave all their votes to the Communist party. Then the Communist militia, composed mostly of Czech workers and lower-income citizens with sickle and hammer bandanas took to the streets and looted and occupied most of the government offices. It was months before everything calmed down.

Charles University, which had been closed to us during the war years, reopened, and I was happy to begin my studies. As I was returning in 1944, after the war had ended, to a more normal life, world politics turned and recovery efforts were underway. Back in Ostrava, my father once again turned his attention to commerce and started to enlarge his meatpacking and cattle businesses with plans to build a large meatpacking factory on land he had bought in a suburb of Prague called Liben. He made sure that I studied business administration as well as law. He was designing our lives as he had ruled before, but there was one thing he had not counted on—that the land he had bought for the expansion had been claimed by the Communist regime. After the death of my mother in 1992 and after the Czech Republic became a democratic country again, the property was returned to me, but since I was not a Czech citizen anymore, I had to assign it temporarily to my distant cousin, Denisa Gregor. My former student employee who came to Tennisport in New York to work for many years to support herself and finish her medical studies. Dr. Marketa Urbanova lives there, and I named it "Tennisport Prague." She is a director of Tennisport Praha. I did not know what else to name it, and it occurred to me that maybe in the future I could open a tennis club there. After the law was changed in favor of original owners, I was able to get the property back and have been busy in America to worry about it.

My university years were enjoyable, evenly split between studying, partying, and dating, a formula I considered well balanced. There were social and political meetings and the opportunity to play tennis, the latter being of greater interest, particularly since I was able to hit a few balls with Jaroslav Drobny, who at that time was also a top ice hockey player. He later became both a national Czech champion and a Wimbledon champion. He and I would play in the seniors United States Championship in Forest Hills in 1962. We lost in the semifinals to Billy Talbert and Gardnar Mulloy.

While I was studying in Prague, I became a member of a club called Friends of USA and of the International Students'

Ball in 1946. I still have my membership card, in fact. We met students from foreign countries, learning about their countries, we entertained them and of course, dated the girls. It was the most exciting life meeting lot of new students after being isolated from outside world for many years. I met student colleague named Sonia, and we dated, a relationship that I thought was going fine until she dumped me for a more attractive man named Vlasta Holecek, who happened to be the European champion in the four-hundred-meter hurdles, a double blow to what little ego I had left. Eventually they married, and years later I met them again by coincidence in Australia, and we continued our friendship. After more years passed, they came to visit us a few times in New York.

Admiring view from President's office

Stealing Identity to Escape

Luckily, the night before escaping one of my friends, Pastusek, had a small party to celebrate the opening of his boutique in town and invited many of our mutual friends, including some girls. It was good cover. Desperate to get to safe ground I needed another ID, because Emil said they had our names and we could be stopped at any train stop on the way to the border. I used the party as an opportunity to take Pastusek's *{kennekarte}* his ID card, out of his coat, which was hanging with many others in the entrance hall. If I had asked him for it, he would have been an accomplice. I didn't tell him and reasoned that he would not miss it for a couple of days. My friends and I assumed the authorities would be looking for those of us who were involved in the march on Hradcany Castle and who were involved in the anti-Bolshevik movement or Friends of USA. Any person who would disagree with Communist doctrine was considered an enemy of the state or a traitor.

No one in Czechoslovakia or Germany could function without these identifications. At Pastusek's party, where there were many new and old friends, one of them Mirek Tvardek, who I knew was also involved in anti-communist activities. He had talked often about the possibility of immigrating to Canada at previous meetings a few months before. When I told him I was leaving for the west the next night, he asked to go with me. "What about your parents?" I asked him. "They are divorced, and I don't live with them anymore," he answered. I agreed to his coming along, and we fled under the cover of darkness, the two of us boarding the night train and heading first to Prague and then to Cheb. This was the closest town to the German border that we could reach by train. The train stopped at numerous control points, where we were asked for our traveling documents and questioned about why we were traveling. Mirek and I replied that we were going to help the farmers in Cheb.

We Made a Successful Crossing Selb- 5km

Wish that this one could have continued to Prague.

It was getting dark when we got to the village of Cheb, which we had never been to before. Getting to the border and across to safety was going to require better directions than I could get from the map in the Atlas that I had, so we decided to rest at an inn that night and wait for early morning, planning to feel out the area and listen to local gossip. Before going to sleep, we went out to buy a few supplies from a nearby shop for the next day's trip. When we returned to the inn, we discovered that the window to our room was open. Luckily for us, we listened for a moment and overheard a conversation between the innkeeper and a policeman as we were entering the inn. It had a small, closed area before the entrance to the lobby, so we stopped there and were not spotted. They were discussing the name Pastusek, the name I registered under. I suspect that either the innkeeper denounced us as suspicious characters or the true owner of the ID, Pastusek, had reported to the police that his ID card had been stolen. Maybe someone at

45

the party also overheard that I intended to escape west and put two and two together with the missing ID. I didn't mention my student situation in Prag to Mirek since he was not involved in our students' march in Prague.

We moved swiftly, turning quietly on our heels and walking west in the dark of night toward what we thought was the border. We struggled through fields and forests most of the night, trying not to be seen. In the train on the way to Cheb we had overheard other passengers saying that in the last forty-eight hours, the Communist regime had doubled its border patrols using dogs. It was rumored that they were shooting at anybody who tried to cross. We heard the dogs barking, and every twig we stepped on made noise. We were scared.

The night felt endless and the trek long and arduous. Every little sound scared us and filled us with the fear of being spotted and captured. Near morning, we emerged from the forest onto a small road and saw a German-style road sign that said, "Selb—5 km." We knew then that we had made it to the West German side of the border. Not knowing what to expect when we crossed, I hid my nine-millimeter pistol under a tree at the edge of the forest and tried to memorize the area where I left it. It was the same gun that I had exchanged for food from our army soldier before the occupation and that was hidden during the Nazi's occupation and again during the communist era. During our trip, I had to have it on my person since the train inspectors looked mostly in the luggage to find any smuggled liquor or food for the black market. It was difficult to part with it since it had stayed with me through the war, always hidden. During the German occupation and the Communist regime, if anyone was caught with a weapon, he could be sentenced to death.

While we were walking toward Selb, we were approached and picked up by American military police in their jeep. As the MP drove us to the station, I realized later that the jeep was made by the firm that made the Whippet. How symbolic it seems now, as if I were being introduced to my new home by these vehicles. The army personnel interrogated us at their military compound and sent us to a nearby German refugee camp that was also for Sudeten German refugees. Administratively, it was in chaos. Mirek was likely sent to a different camp, and we were on our own.

Murder in the Displaced Persons Camp

At that time, the influx of Czech refugees had not yet started. To the Americans, refugees at this point were all the same, and they put us in with Sudeten Germans. This was like putting gasoline on a fire. Most of these Germans had been managers and appointed owners of Czech farms during the war. After the war, they were thrown out, sent to Germany, and put in refugee camps along with those they had ruled. The building was a wooden barrack with about sixty army cots, each with one green army blanket. The room was dark, with only a few windows, and the building was approximately fifty meters long. It was probably used during the Nazi regime to house forced laborers from Poland, Czech Republic, Romania, and anywhere else. It was a very depressing place and became more so as the hundreds of displaced and hungry people who crossed the border searching for safety were rounded up and placed in what was becoming an overcrowded cauldron of contempt and pent-up anger. There was constant hunger. About ten cots were designated as being for the early group of Czech refugees. Next to me was a jeweler by the name of Kriz who was from Prague, and he could not sleep at all because he was afraid he would be robbed. I guessed that he must have had some of the jewelry on him.

One morning, we were horrified to find that, a few cots away, a Czech refugee had been discovered with his throat cut. We guessed that some of the Sudeten Germans recognized him as someone who had taken over their farm when the Czech government nationalized it. The investigation by the German police went nowhere. At that time, the Germans had no rights or organizations willing to be bothered with this small murder, and Americans didn't interfere in Germany's local affairs, so they did not investigate it properly and we didn't hear any more about it. But it was evidence of the rage and hatred between Czechs and Germans immediately after the war. As a young man in the western part of Europe for the first time, everything around me felt strange. I was scared and uncertain about what to expect, I was alone, and hunger and violence was all that I had seen. I had one advantage—the ability to speak German and a little English.

There was very little food available. The Germans didn't even have food for themselves. The only thing we got to eat in the morning was so-called black coffee, and in the afternoon it was so-called Eintopf, or "one-pot stew," which was hot water with a couple of potatoes and cabbage in it. Luckily, four days later, the Americans transferred us to a different refugee camp for Czech student refugees that they had set up near the small town of Schwabach. There were already at least fifty Czech student refugees in army barracks like the one in Selb, and hundreds more were arriving every day to other refugee camps in Ludwigsburg or Frankfurt.

Though many of the refugees were from our university, only a few of us spoke a bit of English, an advantage when interacting with the Americans. But it wasn't the Americans who were in control. The Germans controlled the food supply and housing. And without enough food for even their own people, hunger was our constant companion. Even today, when people speak of the war, it is hunger that comes first to my mind.

Unless you live through something like this, you do not know what hunger is. I went to the village and sold my mother's ring, which I thought I would keep forever, to a Greek who later made it his business to come to the camp every day to buy whatever anyone had to sell. He knew we were desperate, and he had no shame in taking advantage of us. With the meager money I got for the ring, I bought some bread and lard to share with my roommates. With the few marks I had left, I bought a gold bracelet from another student; his mother had given it to him to help him survive. The bracelet was hollow inside, but I filled it with little bit of lead to make it heavier since I didn't think the Greek paid enough for my mother's ring, and I sold the bracelet to him. Afterward, when I was transferred with a few other students to Nuremberg, I heard that he was looking for me.

On the way back from the village, a small dog followed me all the way back to the camp and stayed with us. Everybody loved him. Even when there wasn't much to eat, we always found something to feed the dog. A few days passed when I didn't see him at all, and one evening the colleagues in our quarters invited me for a beef stew. Later, I discovered that my roommate's friends had killed the dog to make the stew. This shows that people who are hungry and desperate will do things that under normal circumstances would be unthinkable. It's called survival.

1949 Pavel Tigrid: "Do Not Have Any Illusions"

A few weeks into our stay in the Schwabach camp, Pavel Tigrid, a Czech journalist living in Paris, arrived. His assignment was to write about life in the camp for a French newspaper. Our student group held several political discussions with him, and we felt elevated at the thought that our opinions were important enough to be listened to by a respected journalist and that our work warranted his attention. We were willing to risk our lives for a mission we believed we were helping our country to win the fight against communist regime. He was in our camp and in our midst, a sure sign that what we were doing truly mattered. Those thoughts were shattered in a flash at the end of one of our political discussions. Tigrid suddenly stopped speaking, stood up on a stool, looked around at the ragtag group of intelligence-gathering volunteers, and said, "Do not have any illusions. Our country is lost to the communists, and we will never return home."

I will never forget the impact of those words, uttered with such powerful force that his conviction left no room for hope that the situation would ever be otherwise. It was a stunning blow. We thought of ourselves not just as students but as patriots whose actions could make a difference for our country. Maybe we were foolish or simply naive. Tigrid's words shot our beliefs down as soundly as bullets fired from a rifle at close range. He later became a well-known journalist in exile and, after the fall of Communism, he became the Minister of Culture for the Czech Republic. He has written several books about this era and his years in exile.

111 Furtherstrasse, Nuremberg across Palace of Justice

A few weeks later, an American army officer came to the camp. He chose twelve of us who spoke a little English to organize a group to help bring refugees across the border from Czechoslovakia to Germany. Every day, driving or walking thru Nuremberg I realized how lucky we had been so far in Czechoslovakia that our cities had not been bombed. When I crossed the border to Selb and then to Schwabach, I found only small villages left in Germany, too insignificant to be bombed. Most of the large cities in Germany had been bombed out. Devastation was everywhere and massive. I walked through Frankfurt and Nuremberg filled with disbelief, numbness, and shock at the sight of mountains of rubble where buildings once stood. I can still see the image of bombed-out buildings, bare, exposed. It felt like looking at human skeletons and I started to realize after meeting with some Germans that not all of them were Nazis and that Hitler committed a crime to them as well. The Army officer moved our students group (about 12 of us) in to a half-bombed-out building at 111 Furtherstrasse in Nuremberg, and despite its condition, we breathed a sigh of relief for the relative security it offered. We closed our eyes without fear of being robbed or attacked or a throat being cut like we had in the refugee camps, where nothing of value was safe. The Germans wore a dismal look of defeat. Their past was catching up with them. In 1939, they had marched into Prague and left many people dead in their wake. Six more years of senseless killing and slaughter took the lives of millions more. Now, photos of Nazi atrocities in concentration camps filled the pages of international newspapers. The world held them accountable.

As this turn of events was unfolding, we were surprisingly close to the heat of the court battle for justice. Our lodging was directly across the street from the Palace of Justice, where the famous Nuremberg Nazi trials were being held.

Our refugee Head Quarters, working for U.S Army in Nuremberg, Furthstrasse 111, in 1948. The right corner on the bottom of photo is the bombed out building where our organization was housed. I think its even our jeep parked before the building. (Photo from Nuremberg Historical Society.)

Emil Ransdorf, as our leader, was to organize safe border passages for political refugees from the Czech Republic and report to our officer who took care of our well-being for finding new ways for crossing the border. It was difficult work. We had to interview and recruit newly arrived refugees from the camps. We had to trust their knowledge of available trails for crossing the border.

We changed trails and routes almost every week as the border situation changed. Every day for few months, using the knowledge gained though our interviews of new refugees, we found new ways to cross the border.

Our lives began to improve when we started getting better food and the use of a jeep. One day, two Army soldiers arrived with two barrels of gasoline for our jeep. We were on the third floor of that bombed-out building. Only Horak, Jansky and Orlicky from our team were downstairs, and one of them shouted up to Emil, "They want me to sign some paper. What shall I do?"

Emil screamed down to him, "Sign President Benes's name, you dumb oxe!" We used one barrel for our official trips, and the second one we sold to better our living standard with food, wine, and cigarettes.

Denson and Rosenthal, Nazi Prosecutors

Just like many coincidences in my life, how could I have known that just across the street, where the Nazi trials were going on, were two men who would reenter my life years later in the United States? One was Robert Rosenthal, a highly decorated pilot in WWII who had flown fifty-two missions over Germany. He graduated as a lawyer and, after the war, as one of the Nuremberg lawyers; he interviewed Hermann Goring, German general Wilhelm Keitel, and others. Much to my surprise, it was he who became my lawyer in New York, handling both my friendly divorce from my first wife and legal matters for my tennis club. Our shared wartime backgrounds in the late 1940s cemented the bond we shared.

The other coincidence was William Denson, a military prosecutor of Nazi war criminals. Between 1945 and 1947, he sent ninety-seven of them to be hung and another eighty to prison. When I moved to Lawrence, Long Island, he became my neighbor and friend who loved to go fishing with me on our ranch in Wyoming. Later he published his memoirs and a book titled "*Justice at Dachau*."

I treasured the friendship of Rosenthal and Denson and mourned their loss when they passed away, Denson at the age of eighty-five and Rosenthal at age eighty-nine, taking comfort in the fact that they led full, rich lives and had achieved important goals. The question of when I will be called next, often comes to my mind.

One of my assignments was to take a VIP, a Czech senator, across the border from Germany to Austria. Being experienced at crossing by train and avoiding capture in previous expeditions, we arrived safely to the city of Innsbruck, where a small group of

Czech refugees was staying at a hotel called the Goldener Hirsch, which means "golden deer" in German. Refugees had formed a Czech government-in-exile at the hotel, information that the senator had gotten from unknown sources. During my three-day stay, one of the Austrian mountain climbers whom I had met in the lobby of the hotel allowed me to accompany him to the top of the Zugspitze. To this day, I still have the picture he took of me under the cross on the top of the mountain. Who would have thought that I would have the opportunity to take the same picture under the same cross with my own sixteen-year-old son when we visited Austria thirty years later?

Our Nuremberg operation ended when one of the refugees told us that the connections in Prague had been taking money from some people to cross the border. So our leader, Emil Ransdorf had a meeting with the Army officer in charge and decided to cease our operations. We all went in different directions. Happy not to go back to D.P. Camps, I wish I had owned a camera that time to show my children the devastation of the era that I and many others lived thru.

Memory from the day

53

Documents Valued as Gold

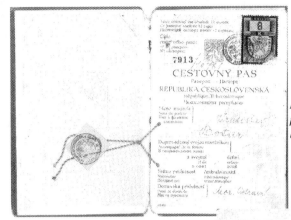

Never had Czech passport, but bought one.

Original Military Travel Document issued by U.S. Army.

I learned how to reconstruct old Swiss passports (this one with my photo and Swiss identity).

Working for the US Army, as civilians did, came with special rights, such as allowing us to use the American and Allied facilities with American ID's. The Germans were not allowed those privileges at all. A $ currency called scripts allowed us to buy things in the PX, or Post Exchange. The ID's also served as currency, official documents, and a passport, entitling us to ride trains and other public transportation free.

When our mission ended in Nuremberg, I sought out a butcher whom my father had told me about before I left home. They may have worked together in the meatpacking plant in Vienna in late 1900. At least I had one name and the hope of a family friend who would welcome me after years of an exhausting war and danger. I hitchhiked my way to Furth, where the butcher lived, about ten kilometers south of Nuremberg. Catching a lift in an Army jeep, I rode with two female officers who worked for Military Special Service in Nuremberg. One introduced herself as Captain Dorothy McKnight, a name that sticks with me to this day. A few days later they invited a colleague from the camp Jansky and me to have dinner with them at a canteen for the US officers, who were extremely polite and kind to us. They offered to give us food but couldn't offer me any kind of a job, so I went to Frankfurt with another name my father had given me: William Heim, a member of one of the old German families, running the Roteschirm, a two-hundred year old sausage and butcher shop. Again, I think it must have been one of the people my father worked with in Vienna. They were very nice and helpful. They rented me a room in their house on Wertheimer Strasse, and this became my temporary base.

I was trying to figure out how to make a living and be able to pay the rent when it occurred to me that, on my travels between Germany and Czech Republic, that some of the train tickets had been paid for by foreigners who used other currencies. On one of my trips, I got acquainted with the conductor on the Orient Express, who was Swiss, and I made him a proposition: I would give him twice the amount for the tickets in Czech crowns for another currency that had more value than crowns.

He destroyed the old slips and redid them all in crowns after finishing his shift, and I gave him double their value in crowns. In exchange, he gave me dollars or other foreign currencies then I bought more Czech crowns and made five times profit on each transaction.

The train went from Switzerland and France, through Germany to Prague. People were still traveling to Prague and very often bought tickets on the train in foreign currency. By this time, thousands of new Czech refugees were moving into the camps every day, and they all needed to exchange Czech crowns, which had no value outside Czechoslovakia to. I handled their transactions for a few months, making good money, and was able to pay my rent to Mrs. Heim. This was the normal way at that time, of course, but it was after the war, when many people could survive only by working the black market. Once other refugees learned of my scheme, they tried to do the same thing, and after a short time, it was no longer profitable. Though I had to forsake currency trading by train, I had soon found another activity which was

Homemade passport for my friend.

charitable, I learned how to create or redo passports for some displaced persons.

Displaced Persons Camp - Ludwigsburg

On one of my trips to refugee camps when I was trying to find out if Mirek or some refugees I had met in Swabach or Selb were in this Ludwigsburg Displaced Person camp, I met Jaroslav Cajka, the son of one of my father's friends. He was trying to immigrate to the United States, and he was very happy to see me. I took him out of the lager (Displaced Person Camp) back to stay with me in Frankfurt. All he needed was a new ID and a passport to get out of Germany in order to get to any democratic country. In those days, passports of any kind—valid or not, real or false, for whatever country—were more valuable than money. People were desperate to get out of the refugee camps, where conditions were terrible. It is so difficult today for me to describe life in those overfilled DP camps. People would immigrate anywhere. It wasn't where they were going that mattered. There was tremendous fear of communism in Europe, and all the refugees who ran away from it were scarred from Russian aggression.

By coincidence, I also met in this camp Dr. Svatopluk Boruvka, a lawyer with whom my father dealt on occasion in Prague planning to expand his business. We kept in touch when he migrated to USA. Years later, when I was in Australia, I asked him for a letter of recommendation so that I could immigrate to the United States. He supplied one, and I was very thankful.

In Frankfurt, I bought an old Swiss passport from the same train conductor who had split the profits of the rail currency operations with me. At that time, passports were not sophisticated, and it was not difficult to change the photo, the stamp, or the data. One of the tricks I used made it easier to transfer official stamps to our new documents. I learned from one of our refugees in camp to use the raw skin from an egg, apply it to the original stamp, and then peel it off to transfer it to our made document. The captains on commercial freight ships accepted any workers with a passport on the ship, merely by looking at the name, passport, stamp, and country of origin before hiring people. There were no background or security checks in those days.

So I made a passport on a piece of stationary for my father's friend's son, Jaroslav Cajka copying the official Czech passport data and attaching his picture. Then I got him across the French border by train to Paris, where we stayed overnight at uncle Charles and then boarded a train to Marseille. There he got a job as cook on a ship that was going to the United States, jumped the ship in Baltimore and applied for political asylum.

From Paris, I returned to Frankfurt and my base at the Heims' house. I was proud to be able to help him. I later received a letter from him when I was in Sydney, saying that before he sailed, he had accidentally met his friend Dusan Klega and they had both sailed on the cargo ship to Baltimore.

I felt very comfortable knowing that I had a Swiss passport for myself under the name Emil Bohlhalter if I ever needed to quickly travel outside of Germany. With that, I could have traveled anywhere, except, of course, to Switzerland. It made me feel secure in my new, foreign environment. I felt more like a free man and less like a refugee, which at that time gave me self-confidence.

When Jaroslav Cajka got to Baltimore, he and his friend Dusan jumped ship, went to the immigration office, and asked for political asylum. He then moved to New York and found employment at the Waldorf Astoria as a chef and two years later he was married and had two children. On his birthday, he gave me the passport I had made for him, which brought back some memories. Thirty years later, his daughter Suzan worked at my Tennisport club and later then moved to Florida, where her ailing mother lived. Her younger brother moved to somewhere in the Caribbean Islands, and she didn't hear from him for a few years. Jaroslav Cajka, unfortunately, died when he fell asleep behind the wheel of his car after working a night shift. The only other friend who could tell the story of the trip on the ship from Marseille is Dusan Klega, who lives in California and became an actor. I have not been in touch with him for many years, but recently I found out from his wife, Doris, that he has not been well. I should have asked Jerry or Dusan years ago about their ship experience. Years pass very fast when you work hard, and back then I wasn't thinking about my memoir.

I saw so many refugees and so much misery. Looking back, it seems like a bad dream, but it was not. At times, it is hard to digest or reconcile that I had lived through it all and emerged intact, including my father's deserting the family and then returning to discipline us, which seemed hard at the time. But that was soft compared with what I lived through later, especially the Russian and Nazi atrocities that forced everyone to survive by their own grit and agility. I am both proud of and mystified at the memories. There are nightmares, like helping others survive in a bunker in our home only to see one of the occupants, an innocent one-armed man, flee for his life and, after he fled, the brutal rape that destroyed his wife. I remember my personal deeds for sheer survival: I created false passports to help strangers escape to freedom, sold the ring my mother had given me, and unknowingly ate a dog that had been slaughtered because there was great hunger. No one, even those of us who had been raised with privilege in Eastern Europe, whose childhoods included violin, piano lessons and tennis and operas, concerts etc., would ever recover without the scarring that only war and cruelty can leave. Everywhere the war had been, it left a trail of destruction. Buildings blew up, and lives blew apart.

When I think of the Czech refugees whose lives I touched and who touched my life during those days of intense political and economic struggle, so many of the memories find their way back to my room at Mrs. Heim's house, which became a safe haven for some people, including Zdenek Capek, an engineer, and his friend Zelenda. Both were looking for shelter, and I took them into my room, with Mrs. Heim's permission. Zelenda had run the largest heavy-machinery manufacturing business in Czechoslovakia before being nationalized. With their combined engineering genius and manufacturing skills, the two men built a prototype of a mini-car by hand in Mrs. Heim's of their time. I still have a picture of this wonderful minicar. Capek and Zelenda later managed to immigrate to Ethiopia, where they became engineers and advisors to Emperor Haile Selassie for the King Solomon's mines. A few years later, they immigrated to the United States and became successful industrialists. We kept in touch by mail while I was in Sydney. Capek gave me the two reels of eight-millimeter film shot about mining in Solomon mines during his years in Ethiopia, though the film may have deteriorated. It was thanks to the kind heart of Mrs. Heim that I was able to use my room for them to live in and the garage for them to build their mini-car in. Her home was a refuge for my friends during those turbulent times.

Capek, fifty years ahead of his time.

Bailed Out by Uncle in Paris

I have been in contact with refugee organizations—for other refugees in Frankfurt, though it turns out that not all of them were as pure of soul and purpose as Zelenda and Capek. There were many shady characters among the DP-camp people, including some safecrackers, who were sent by mistake to a refugee camp in Italy. One day, while still in Nuremberg visiting and inquiring about the situations and conditions with refugees, I was approached by a French officer from the Deuxieme Bureau. He asked me to pass along any information I found out about new refugees who might have been placed in the Schwabach or other DP camps by the Communists because they were already sending their spy cells to establish a person's credibility as a political refugee. After they immigrated to other countries, they would become spies. The officer's name was Monsieur Dubois. He told me he had an office in Strasbourg. "Any time you need something, do not hesitate to give me a call," he said, and he gave me his telephone number. I had the occasion to do so later only to discover how insincere that offer of help really was.

Two other roommates who also slept on thin mattresses on the floor of my room were Krykorka, who had been an exporter of glass and jewelry in Jablonec, and Kostelecky, who claimed to be an importer and exporter in Prague. Kostelecky later immigrated to New York City and did all kinds of jobs, including teaching tennis in my club. He was a heavy smoker, and he died in the 1980s of lung cancer. Krykorka was a well-to-do guy who later migrated to Argentina and had a small suitcase of zircons—aquamarines, rubies, and diamonds. I bought some of his glass bijouterie, which I knew I could sell in France for triple the price, and I put it in a suitcase. I planned to travel to Strasbourg and Paris to sell it. I had made this trip several times before, bringing somebody over the border without documentation, so I was confident.

Unfortunately, at the border in Kiehl, which is the last stop before the French border, an officer asked me, "Do you have anything to declare?" In all the times I had traveled this route, no one had ever asked about my luggage. I think that I looked cocky or answered, "no" in a cocky way, so he asked, "What do you have in that suitcase?" "I am a Czech refugee," I said. "This is the only property that I was able to save from being confiscated by the government." It didn't work. Perhaps he was a French Communist. He asked me to go with him to the office, which was about fifty meters away from the train. At that time, there were still many places without electricity in the towns and villages that had been bombed or damaged. The officer's room had about four petrol lamps, and that was it. I entered and saw two gendarmes and another customs clerk. I had to open the suitcase. Can you imagine the impact when I opened it in that light and all those aquamarines, diamonds, and rubies appeared? The gendarmes drew their guns. They thought they had just caught the biggest jewelry smuggler of all time. I tried to explain that the jewels were not real, that they were made of glass, but they would not believe it. They put me in the local jail with some drunk. The cell was about four by four meters, with an open hole in the corner for the toilet. In the morning, the chief came in and declared that the jewels were, in fact, made of glass. But they still fined me a huge sum in French francs. I was allowed to call Monsieur Dubois in Strasburg, the French officer I had met at the refugee camp who told me to call him if I ever needed anything. I asked him to help me out, but he told the police he had never heard of me. Of course, my last contact with him had been about a year earlier and I was not able to help with information he asked for.

Broke again and nearly out of ideas, I had one number left to call—that of my uncle in Paris, Charles Pachta. He was my mother's brother and a very well-known celebrity tailor on Avenue Victor Hugo in Paris. He bailed me out, but the police confiscated the suitcase and its contents. So, once again, I had lost everything. When I arrived in Paris, my uncle did not receive me cheerfully. He tolerated me for three days but then told me to leave. He refused to give me a single franc. Through our refugee organization called IRO, I knew of an American-Czech businessman named Richard Vogel whose office was used by IRO [International Refugee Organisation} people to help displaced persons. I managed to locate and visit him at the Grand Hotel, where he had his temporary office, and he gave me a twenty-dollar loan, which was enough to get me back to Frankfurt because I had to pay only for the train ticket from Paris to the German border, and from there I traveled by using my army or other documents. By the time I got back to Germany, I hadn't eaten all day and didn't have a penny. I went back to Mrs. Heim's only to hear her say that I could no longer stay there. Her daughter was expecting a baby and she would need the room. I understood at that very moment what it is to feel desperate—truly desperate. I had no money, only the food that Mrs. Heim gave me, and a few more days with a place to stay. And I could not pay her the rent I owed. I had exhausted the list of names my father had given me, and I had sold the gold ring my mother gave me in Schwabach. I had nothing left for company but hunger, a future as a homeless foreigner, without a pfennig. Destitute, I walked the bombed-out city streets of Frankfurt aimlessly, thinking of returning to one of the DP camps, where hundreds of others just like me awaited the same uncertain future. Somehow, I shared in a small way the city's horrible conditions: flattened, shattered, bombed-out, depressed.

Though I was broke and hungry, I had one advantage—the documents left from my work with the Americans opened the doors to places reserved for Army personnel, people who worked for the American or Allies' embassies or consulates. There in heart of the bombed Frankfurt, I saw a sign marking a premise reserved for Americans and Allies. I pulled out my wrinkled papers and entered.

I had walked into the Palmengarten, a beautiful park in Frankfurt. In the middle of the park was a grand-looking clubhouse with a terrace, and in front of it were five red clay tennis courts. It reminded me of the courts at home.

And right there, on that day—and without my realizing it—my life changed forever, there must of have been somebody in heaven, an angel in the form of a caretaker and asked:

Chapter Three:
"Mister, Do You Play Tennis?"
The question which changed
my life forever in 1948.

At that time of day, the Palmengarten Tennis Club was deserted. I found a place to sit and rest overlooking the courts. I thought, *"What a waste. Nobody is on them."* Not long after I sat down, a gentleman who looked to be in his sixties walked over from the clubhouse. He came over to me and asked me politely in German, "Mister, do you play tennis?" Yes, I play a little bit, I replied. "If you could do me a favor," he said. "There is an American army captain who is looking for someone to play with." He introduced himself as the caretaker of the club. I told him that I did not have tennis clothes or a racket with me, so he took me to the locker room and got me a pair of shorts and an old racket. I walked out onto the court, and minutes later, a soldier in a US captain's uniform arrived. He was very short and bald, and he kept two Doberman pinschers tied up at the next tennis court. He introduced himself as Captain Atlas.

Turning pro. Palmagarten, Frankfurt, 1948.

I found out after a few days that Captain Atlas managed all the post exchanges (PXs), stores where Allied soldiers and their families could buy everything from food to clothing and household items. We played for an hour, and he seemed to enjoy himself very much. As soon as we finished, he asked me to play again the next day. Then he handed me two scripts, legal $ currency for American soldiers and other Allied persons in occupied Germany. He must have been under the impression that I was a club pro. It was manna from heaven. With these scripts, I could buy whatever I needed: nuts and bolts or diamond rings. I was able to go to a PX snack bar inside Palmengarten Park and within walking distance from the tennis club. I got a full meal with coffee for 80 cents and candy for another 20 cents. I also bought a carton of cigarettes for one dollar, which I later took downtown and sold for about thirty deutsche marks. At that time, the exchange rate was fifteen marks to a dollar, so I had my two dollars back and then some. That was a very good day.

The groundskeeper at the club told me that a number of high-ranking British, American, and French nationals had offices right around the corner at IG Farben building and that they often asked him if there were someone around to hit with. Since all Allied personnel were automatically members of the tennis club and were always looking for a game, like Captain Atlas, I received a letter from US Army headquarters, Special Service Division, permitting me to teach there as a non-salaried employee whenever I liked and to charge for the time. It was my mother who had insisted that I take lessons as a fourteen-year-old, but it was the war that turned my life upside down and landed me in a foreign country with a groundskeeper, who accidentally gave me my start in a tennis career. The ingredients came together into an unlikely recipe for a lifetime of rich experiences, incredible travel, and interesting people.

Within a few days, I was giving four to six lessons a day at three dollars per hour and using the money to buy and sell merchandise from PXs. Life started to look rosy.

Commissioner for Germany, John McCloy

One of the first people I played with was John McCloy, the US High Commissioner of Occupied Germany, one of those high-ranking officials with an office at IG Farben around the corner. McCloy heard that there was finally somebody at the club who could hit a few balls, so he became a regular student. Twenty-five years later, his grandson, John McCloy III, became a good friend of my son, Freddie, at the Brooks School in the States. After my dismissal, he wrote a letter expressing his regret over my departure from the River Club, where he was a member and took more lessons from me when I was there, as a pro that time. What a coincidence it was meeting him again decades later in New York.

Even on the court, intrigue played a role. One of my new pupils was a pretty woman named Renee, secretary to the French consul, Messier DeCamp. A few months later, at my request, Messier DeCamp who was also my new client let Renee, whom I had dated for a few weeks; go to Prague with me under official pretenses. The real reason for the trip was to get a letter to Prague for my mother with information on where I was and what I was doing, since the communists censored all the mail. I didn't want Renee to carry the letter, so I put it behind the framed picture in her first class train compartment. She never had the chance to recover it. She told me that two gentlemen boarded the train, sat next to her, and took it upon themselves to be her protectors, insisting that they share their cab with her and see her safely to her hotel in Prague. With only three minutes to disembark before the train would pull out of the station and leave her stranded, she was afraid to try to beat the clock and return to the cabin. The framed picture with the hidden letter rode on with the train.

While in Palmengarten, I taught or met people whose paths would cross mine again in the decades to come. Some had tennis careers that I would follow all the way from the days of radio to days of tennis matches streaming live on a laptop. There was Willy Messerschmitt, who had been on the German Davis Cup team before 1936. We met when he opened the first sports store in

Place that changed my life— Frankfurt Palmengarten, 1948. "Mister do you play tennis?"

My first tennis team at Palmengarten Tennis Club incld. my first wife, second from the left, and myself at the end of the group on the right beside French Consul DeCamp.

Frankfurt. There were the Schambachs, who owned a textile shop and had a very pretty daughter whom they wanted me to marry, a proposition that I considered for a few minutes. My guess is that they probably knew that, as a Czech refugee who had worked for the Allies, I had documents entitling me to emigrate, and they wanted to get her out of the country safely; doing so was very difficult for Germans after the war. At that time as tennis teacher for Americans, I was considered to be doing well but was not interested in marriage, let alone a marriage of convenience. I was allowed to bring a few Germans into Palmengarten, and they happily paid double for the honor of playing in the American-type environment, hoping as well to exchange marks for dollars or other currencies. I became an instant success in the American and Allied social circles, being invited to parties and dinners. After fourteen days, the tennis terrace was suddenly full of people waiting for a court opening and a social gathering.

Army Officer, Margie Schaefer

My collection of Army Insignias.

Even if I had not considered the prospect of spiriting the Schambachs' daughter to a non-occupied country, there was another player who had caught my attention, an attractive young lady wearing a United States Army uniform. Her name was Margie Schaefer. After a few lessons, we had a cup of coffee, and in conversation she mentioned that she and a few other officers had the privilege of having an audience with the Pope few days ago at the Vatican. Everybody was kissing his ring, she said, but when it was her turn she was so overwhelmed by all the surroundings that she shook his hand. I was impressed by her courage and individuality, and we started to date.

As a US Army officer, she had been assigned a beautiful villa that the Allies had confiscated from the Germans. It was on the corner of Palmengarten Park, just about a five-minute walk from the tennis courts. I asked if there was a room to rent there, and the rest is history. Margie told me that she had been born in Luxemburg, and when the first units of the American army liberated her country, she enlisted as an interpreter with the US troops. She was multilingual, able to speak English, French, Spanish, Italian, Russian, and later Czech. She then started learning Mandarin because of C. V. Starr's influence on our trips to Hong Kong. She held a very good position in the offices of IG Farben, where the high commissioner, US Army, and other offices were housed. After a few lessons and starting to get to know each other, Margie explained to me the difficulties that her family faced during the war in Luxembourg because of their last name. Schaeffer-Loeb sounded Jewish, but I never asked her for details. She also had a brother and a sister living in Brussels. Margie and I became very good friends, and after two months, on February 3, 1949, we were married in the local army chapel. Word spread around the colony of Czech refugees in nearby camps that Freddie Botur, married to an army officer, had struck it rich. In fact, we were just beginning to live comfortably by the deprived standards of the day, but with all things being relative, Czech refugees started to visit the club daily, asking me to help them out. Our comfortable lifestyle allowed me to buy my first car, a secondhand Buick. In the trunk, I built a large gas tank, so that I could sell gas to Germans for double the price I had paid; as an Allied person. More importantly, I was beginning to experience the democracy of the Western way of life, with few restrictions, and my new appetite for a better quality of life began to grow.

After our wedding, attended by Margie's mother and brother from Luxemburg, and her very good friend Margaret from the British consulate, we started to discuss the opportunity to immigrate to the United States. I had priority since I was an employee for a short time in the US office section. I wanted to continue my studies in the States, but Margie was more adventurous. She wanted to move to Australia, and I agreed. It sounded good to me, especially since the Australian government would pay for the trip if we signed a two-year contract to do whatever government work they assigned. Margie and I had to wait a week for her dismissal from the Army barracks in Wurzburg.

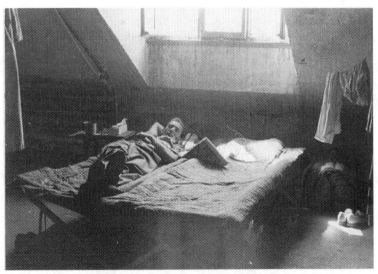

Waiting in Wurzburg Army compound for Margie's release from the army before leaving for Australia which had similarity of the first displaced persons camp in Selb

The night before Margie and I were to leave for Bremerhaven to begin our trip to Australia, I suggested that we celebrate. I wanted to take my bride out for a good dinner at the Baden-Baden Casino. We had already sold the car but were allowed to use it until the day of our departure. So with the profit from the car sale and our savings, we were getting ready to start our new life in Australia with more than five thousand dollars. Out of that, I took two hundred dollars and had Margie hide the rest while we went to the casino. As we left our room, I caught a reflection of her putting the money in a jar. We went out to the car, and I started the engine. "Wait a moment. I have to go to the toilet," I said. Once inside, I dipped into the jar for another two hundred dollars as a reserve—just another two hundred because I loved to gamble. When I reached nervously for the jar, it fell on the floor and broke. I saw all the bills lying there, and in a hurry, I shoved the hundred-dollar-bill rolls into my pockets and did not say anything to Margie.

We had a wonderful dinner with some of her friends, whom I had invited. We played a few games of poker and hit the slot machines. Margie came to me and said she had lost my hundred dollars.

"Don't worry. I've been winning," I lied as I handed her another hundred. She came back a few more times like this. Some time went by, and I realized that I was down to our last three hundred dollars. I played baccarat and hit the bank. Then I had almost four thousand, but that still didn't cover my losses. Margie and our friends who joint us for dinner were pulling my arm, telling me to take it—take it and quit. But no! I found out then what it meant when gamblers say they have gambling fever, that they cannot hear or see. Of course, I lost everything.

"What a great pity," Margie said. "We could have added another four thousand dollars to our account."

We drove home in silence. Margie said what a wonderful evening it was, especially when I hit the bank with four thousand on. My heart was in my stomach, knowing that it was just a matter of time until Margie found out the truth. When we walked in the door, she saw the broken jar on the floor. There wasn't much to explain, but at least she didn't ask right away for a divorce. The next day, she got her sister to wire us five hundred dollars from Brussels so we could go on the trip to Bremerhaven. That was a lesson that I'll never forget, and since then, gambling has never excited me. If I go to the casino, I bet five or ten dollars and walk away. My father had been a big gambler, and I should have remembered the toll it took on our family. Some genes, I realized, were better discarded, and hard lessons, I learned, can be expensive, but they stick with you.

Staff Sergeant, Herbert Zeese

We left for Bremerhaven by train, and when we arrived, we discovered that our ship to Melbourne had been delayed. We would not sail for three months. Since we both had Allied papers, but very little money, I went to the Bremerhaven Country Club, which was similar to Frankfurt's Palmengarten Club and only for Allied and Americans, to see if I could earn money teaching tennis. The club had beautiful red clay courts, a golf course, and horseback riding and was much more elaborate than the one in Frankfurt. I went to the main office and asked for the manager, and the soldier at the entrance pointed me in the right direction. I knocked on the door and saw what looked like a scene from an army movie made in Hollywood. Behind the desk was a staff sergeant with his feet on the desk and a cigarette dangling from his lips. I asked him if I could teach tennis to the Allies in the area while I was waiting for our ship to leave. He looked like a jolly good fellow, with a relaxed smile on his face. "If you can teach me, you can teach here," he said. His name was Staff Sergeant Herbert Zeese.

We had a cup of coffee, and he showed me around the club. I gave him his first lesson that day and continued after that almost every day of our waiting for our departure. We also had good times with a few glasses of beer. The sergeant was an enthusiastic learner, and I also gave a few lessons over the next few months to people working for the army and occasionally to German players. Altogether, I made enough money to pay for food until my departure. In the meantime, Margie also played as much as she could with local players, serving as my public relations person. During my stay, I got in touch with one of the top German players, as I had in Frankfurt, and told him that he could take my place teaching the sergeant when I left. The sergeant was very happy about it. We said good-bye, never considering that we might see each other again. At last, Margie and I left for Australia to begin the next chapter in our lives.

Australia, 1950: The SS Nelly, Thirty-One Days to Melbourne

The SS Nelly sailing with approximately 1,000 refugees

If we harbored thoughts that setting sail to our new lives in Australia aboard the *SS Nelly* would be romantic and glamorous, those thoughts were quickly dashed. No word in the Czech or English language adequately describes the crashing waves, seasickness, foul odor, and over-crowding with thousands of refugees from different nations and languages. From the hour we left Bremerhaven until we landed just over a month later, it was a voyage best forgotten.

Not long after we left Bremerhaven, close to the coast of Portugal, we encountered a huge storm in the Bay of Biscay, a region known for its fierce weather and storms that have claimed hundreds of lives. In 2009, I read of the crossing of the *"Independence of the Seas"* when doors to decks were locked to keep passengers safe as the ship made its way through the Bay of Biscay's forty-foot seas. During our voyage, we all thought the ship would sink. The waves finally subsided, and we rounded from Gibraltar to Naples, where we loaded more refugees from DP camps in Italy. It was not a large ship, and I spent most of the thirty-one-day crossing feeling like I had been jammed onto a cattle ship. I was seasick and able to eat only bread and fruit, except for when we arrived in one of the ports on the way. Throughout the ordeal, Margie took care of me, maybe thinking my pain was more than just punishment for my losing all of our savings in a single night's gambling spree.

Naples - Port Said, Aden Colombo

From Naples, we went to Egypt's Port Said, where we stayed in port for twelve hours before going through the Suez Canal. Margie was designated as the ship's security officer because of her army background and language skills and received a better bunk bed. Arab merchants in small boats surrounded our ship, trying to sell us their wares. For half an hour, I haggled and bargained with a merchant, finally trading my beautiful portable radio that I had bought at a PX in Bremerhaven for a beautiful Persian Buchara carpet. I kept that rug for nearly fifty years, until one of our dogs damaged it and we had to throw it out.

Despite the continuous cartwheels in my stomach, one other memory stands out. I shall never forget my first sight of a body of water that stretched as far as the eye could see. I had lived all of my life in landlocked Czechoslovakia. I had never experienced such openness. Seeing on the horizon that vast body of water lifted my spirits momentarily, but it offered brief respite from the nausea that dominated and settled in to stay for the most of length of the voyage. With every wave, my stomach heaved. With every roll, I had momentary visions that death must be easier. I thought this must be punishment for my sins.

The ship stopped in Aden to refuel, and then the trip dragged. I cannot remember how many days we traveled to Columbo in Cylon (known today as Sri Lanka), where we were allowed to disembark. In a flash, I saw a new world with people who looked at it through different eyes. Part of the experience was simply the heat. For the first time in my life, I soaked my feet in the ocean that was a temperature of about eighty degrees. It felt like a warm bathtub. We were allowed to leave the ship and told to return by sunset. For the first time, I saw how the British lived in colonies that they had influenced and still ruled with stiffness. Their officers walked very straight and carried their walking canes under one arm, like I have seen in the movie "*Gunga Din.*" For the first time, I saw ancient temples adorned in gold, built with probably thousands of laborers and artists. I saw Indian culture and Buddhism, both of which were completely foreign to me. Everything felt very exotic. We stayed for thirty-six hours, long enough go into the town of Colombo and see a few Buddhist temples, where their religion was explained to us.

Jakarta – Perth, Melbourne

Over the next few days, we sailed to Jakarta in Indonesia and stayed for twenty-four hours, during which we were able to explore the surrounding area. For us Europeans, it was shocking to see people washing in the canal and using it as a toilet at the same time. It was an unbelievable experience hearing from some of the crew about all the exotic islands surrounding the port. Despite the natural beauty, most of the people there were extremely poor, and there seemed to be no end to the poverty we saw in port. We continued our seemingly endless trip to Perth, in Southwestern

Australia, where we had again one full day in port to visit the British Lloyd's registered ship next to us. While walking in the harbor with Margie, I saw a man and a woman with their bags walking on the other side, about forty meters away. Somehow the man's gait seemed familiar.

"Karel!" I called out. The man turned around. It was Karel Fiala, who had been a clerk with the Czech consulate in Frankfurt. He was a passenger on the ship next to us and was on his way to Australia to work as a representative for Underwood Corporation. While he was working for the Czech consulate, he had promised about ten refugees with expired Czech passports that he would extend their passports. He took their money and passports but never extended a single one. For some, the passport was their only possession and their only hope to leave the refugee camp and immigrate to a country that would accept them. "You're lucky it's me and not one of the people whom you disappointed," I said. "I did nothing wrong," he retorted, trying to persuade me that the money was stolen by the concierge at the hotel where he had left the passports and which served as the residence for the Czech consulate. He confessed that he was under suspicion but insisted that the passports left with the concierge were eventually returned to the owners. He maintained his innocence. What a coincidence it was to meet a person I knew in the middle of the globe.

Finally, after thirty-one days on the water, we disembarked in Melbourne harbor, where we have been transferred to the train arriving small town Bonegilla, to a camp for the people whose passage had been paid by the Australian government in exchange for two years of labor. The employment officer divided us into groups and assigned us numbers for our metal Quonset huts, where we would be staying. What a disappointment in our immigration. And what could we expect next?

Sydney, 1950

Sydney in the 1950s

Again, the weather affected our lives. During the day, it was a hundred degrees; at night, it was very cold. After a week, the so-called employment officer sent different groups of us to different cities. A week later, Margie and I were lucky to be assigned to an employment officer in Sydney. When we arrived, we stayed in a boarding house with many other people. I went to the employment officer, and he assigned me the job of laborer at a steel company in an area where the steel axles were made for cars. It was backbreaking labor in intense heat. Since the steel barrels were full of oil, we had to slide white-burning axles into them, vertically, very quickly so they would not catch fire. I did as I was told, or so I thought, but somehow the barrel caught fire and blew up, and I was fired. Thanks to a government protection and our contract I was allowed to remain on the job for another three days, sweeping the floors and being paid.

Back at the employment center in Sydney, we met many other Czechs who had entered Australia the same way we had, getting free passage in exchange for labor. Margie, who was fluent in so many languages, was assigned to quite a good job in the offices of a large Lloyds Shipping company near the Sydney Harbor. Another Czech migrant named Hlavacek and I were assigned to Gorden and Gotsch, a newspaper and magazine distributor. We were paid seven pounds a week to work from eight to five, hauling heavy sacks of printed material, books, magazines, and papers in the basement of the building. Hlavacek stood on one side and I stood on the other, filling the bags with books and magazines to be shipped and an Australian man who could hardly read or count watched over us as our boss. If the first job was frightening because of having to handle burning hot axles in burning hot weather, the second was backbreaking work with no reward or incentive in sight. I needed to find a way to secure better work.

After a week or so, I learned from a reliable source that if I put a five-pound note into a pack of cigarettes and left it on the employment officer's desk, he would give me almost any job I wanted. It worked! Having read in the help wanted section in the local newspaper that cooks were paid twenty pounds a week, I lied to the officer and said that I had been a cook in Czechoslovakia. He gave me a job at the Hotel Australia beginning at fifteen pounds a week, which was twice as much as I had been getting at the beginning.

That was when the difficulties started. When I arrived at 5 a.m. on my first day, I entered the biggest kitchen I had ever seen. People were running in and out, and I felt helpless. I finally found somebody wearing a tall white cap, so I thought he must be the boss. I told him I was the new cook, but since my English was not very good and he had a thick Australian accent, I could hardly understand what he said.

"Don't you see in that corner there is commissary? You go there, change your clothes, and prepare three hundred buns by six o'clock!" he screamed at me and left.

There I was, in striped pants, with a white cook's hat on. I went up to the man in charge of supplies and asked for the ingredients needed to make three hundred buns. "What do I know about buns?" "That's your problem, mate." the man said. His Aussie accent was the least of my worries. And those worries were starting to mount, beginning with figuring out exactly what buns they were looking for and how to make them. I hadn't a clue.

Of course, I knew what buns were. I had seen them in shops. I just tried to remember how my mother had made *buchticky* which are something like jelly doughnuts or cakes. I remembered that she used butter, milk, flour, and eggs, so I just improvised and put everything in a big, round kettle that I greased inside with butter. I started to make some dough, but it was not so easy. After a few minutes, the dough was thick. I added milk, but that turned the batter to soup, so I added flour. Back and forth I went—milk and flour, flour and milk. Finally it was so thick and full to the top that the mixing machine's motor started smoking and burning. The chef ran over to me. "What are you doing here you X...?" he yelled. "Well, we do buns differently in Czechoslovakia," I said. He knew then that I was not a cook, so he put me in the back of the kitchen to peel potatoes and wash the dishes. Thankfully, at that time in Australia, once a company hired a person who was in the country on a government contract, it could not fire him for three days, the same rule that allowed me to stay on sweeping floors or after blowing up equipment in the steel factory. So I peeled potatoes and cut vegetables for three days. In the meantime, I looked around the kitchen to see if I could learn something.

The fourth day, I went back to the employment officer again with another cigarette pack with another five pounds in it. "They did not like my Czech cooking," I said with a straight face. He gave me another job in another hotel, where I would run around doing as little as possible and watching the kitchen operations. I was amazed to see the old cook bent over a dish into which he was hand-mixing some food, and his perspiration was dripping into the dish. I wasn't sure if sweat was one of the ingredients. That time, I lasted a week before they threw me out. But during the evenings, Margie and I read cookbooks and practiced cooking at home. At least I understood meat because of my time around my father's meatpacking business. My cooking experience was improving on account of my government contract. Next, I took a job cooking in a maternity hospital with thirty beds, and that lasted until the day I served *vepro-knedlo-zelo*: pork, cabbage, and dumplings. All thirty dishes came back untouched. People can learn a lot in six months. But, when that person is young, he or she also learns to be adventurous and a little arrogant. So on my next trip to the employment officer, I put twenty pounds in with the cigarettes and told him that in the Czech Republic, I had been running bigger operations than the little placements he was giving me. I said that he would be better off having me manage a restaurant or kitchen. The bribe worked, and I got a job as chef. At that time, Australia was lacking skilled labor, so people could say that they knew this or that skill and nobody would test them.

As they say, "Money can buy almost anything." I introduced myself to the manager of the hotel, who was a Hungarian emigrant, and presented him my credentials from the employment officer, saying I would become a chef at the Hotel Manly at Manly Beach, which was a small hotel in the bay close to a cliff and overlooking the ocean. I had two cooks under me, writing menus and ordering supplies. With others were doing the cooking, the managing part was easy to handle. After all, I had come from a business background and had learned fast during my previous cooking jobs. This position gave me more time to play tennis. Around Christmas time, I also tried making miniature Christmas trees from very large pine cones, to which I added little candles. The plan was to sell them in stores, but it was a fiasco. I think I made fifty and sold three.

Meeting Harry Hopman

In those days in 1950th Sydney was a relatively small, manageable city. The tallest building was the New South Wales Bank, at seven stories high. It was in stark contrast to what I found when I returned thirty years later: skyscrapers and harbor development reminiscent of San Francisco. But with its neighborly feel back then, it was easy to join the action at the local tennis courts, and being invited to play for the local team. During one of the many afternoon teas that followed play, I learned that the famous coach Harry Hopman was training Lew Hoad, Marvin Rose, Rosewall and other top Australian players daily at the White City tennis courts. The players were looking for practice partners and hitters, two people hitting in short intervals to the player. I jumped at the opportunity and hit as often as possible with tournament players.

The first tournament I ever played was at the White City grass courts, on the center court, in a match against Frank Sedgman. I lost soundly—love, love, and one. Another Aussie experience was in a local tournament against Adrian Quist, former singles champion and Davis Cup player. I will never forget his drop shots. He chased me all over the court, and after the match, we shook hands and he said, "Not too bad, young man."

As close as I could get to the Davis Cup, Sydney. 1950.

Harry Hopman, visiting me at RC.

Sedgman whom I played Tennis with in the 1950's in Sydney, Drysdale, myself and Laver at Tennisport

The White City courts experience provided invaluable training. Australia was the hotbed of tennis, producing some of the world's best players and home to year-round activity. And if my cooking wasn't improving, at least my tennis was. During one of those afternoon practice sessions was when I was introduced to Harry Hopman. He was known as a very disciplinary coach and not as friendly, but maybe because I was a Czech refugee, he became friendly. Our friendship was revived later in the United States when Bill Talbert and Harry would come to practice with the players on the grass courts at the Rockaway Hunting Club courts before the Forest Hills championship. The last time Harry, came to visit me with his wife, Lucy, was for a Tennisport charity tournament with John McEnroe, Bjorn Bork, Peter Fleming, Ilie Nastasi, and many other celebrities. My friendship lasted from 1949 until Harry, the man who had been coach to twenty-two Australian Davis Cup teams, passed away in 1985.

During my coaching years in New York, when I could not go to Hong Kong to play with C. V. Starr (Founder of AIG and a major philanthropist) at Christmas time, because I had been taking too many days off from the River Club, Starr asked me to recommend Harry as my replacement. Starr often had business appointments with top government officials from Hong Kong, the Philippines, or Japan who were good tennis players. My friendship with Starr has always been one of the highlights of my life. Little did I know in my early days as a "chef" in Sydney, who played tennis as a hobby that we would become such close friends or that Harry would be asking me for a referral to be a coach for Starr and his friends in Hong Kong. When Starr returned to New York from his Hong Kong trip, he told me that he had had a good time with Harry, who had worked him hard, and had learned a lot. Unfortunately, from this trip he came down with a terrible cold that was later diagnosed as emphysema, from which he never recovered.

Between being fired from the steel-hardening factory and then from hotels and a maternity ward as a cook, there was always a weeklong to ten-day interval before a new job started. During one of the intervals, a friend of mine from Czechoslovakia thought there was good money to be made in trucking logs. We leased a truck and calculated that we could make a hundred pounds per trip from the Blue Mountains Forest about two hundred miles south of Sydney. On about the third trip, we drove the truck up a very steep hill. Suddenly, the logs' weight started to shift, and we jumped out of the truck just in time to save ourselves from being rolled over by the truck and the logs. We were lucky that we had not been crushed, but it was another brief encounter with entrepreneurship that ended without success.

In Sydney, we met many European immigrants who were former doctors, businessmen, sportsmen, or professionals with specialties in biotechnical fields. One was a friend of mine from Prague named Vlasta Holecek. He was one of those men who seemed to have it all—he was a four-hundred-meter hurdles champion and a once- successful businessman in Czechoslovakia who had married a former girlfriend of mine named Sonya and had two children with her. Holecek's business was specializing in gold products in Sydney. He worked out of his apartment and told me that I could do the same working for him, setting marquisate stones into silver watch casings at home in the evenings. He went so far as to show Margie and me how to do it, and the work turned out to be a great boost for our incomes in those days. I still have one of those casings as a souvenir. A few years after we left, Holecek became wealthy by exploiting a tax loophole he discovered in the movement of gold products between England and Australia. He learned that he did not have to pay taxes on the bracelets, rings, and necklaces he made if he declared them as unfinished products. His son became a doctor in Sydney and his daughter was running a hobby farm in Queensland. We have kept in touch for many years.

Joe Hlavacek and his wife became good friends after we met on our first job at Gordon and Gotsch. They wanted to learn to play tennis, so I started them on the local courts. Joe was a successful businessman in forest products in his former country,

Czechoslovakia, and emigrated the same year as Margie and I did. I started to teach him and his wife in Sydney, and when we left Australia he continued playing. Some ten years later, he and his wife, Rose, moved from Australia to Arizona, where he taught tennis at one of the local clubs for many years. He was one of many other Czechs who saw the opportunities in tennis teaching, and I gave him a start in a new country.

After moving to the States, I taught a few other Czechs like Hlavacek about my teaching methods and about tennis as an employment opportunity: Oleg Zabrodsky (a top national hockey player), Kostelecky, Pepa Malecek (a top soccer and hockey player for the national team—a legend in his time), Stan Nepomucky (Nielsen; also a national hockey player), Jansky (also a hockey player), and others who were not great players but through tennis connections became successful in business.

Suad Rizvanbegovic and Christian Cee got good positions through our member of Tennisport, Ted Forstmann. Four-time Czech national champion and Wimbledon semifinals player, Jitka Volavkova, was in great demand for her quality and psychology of tennis. There were also others whose names I cannot remember.

Years later at the River Club, one of the members, H. V. Kaltenborn, a journalist well known for his reporting of World War I, asked me if I knew a pro who could teach at his club on Long Island. I was able to recommend Oleg Zabrodsky, a former national hockey player who had just immigrated to the States, was looking for a job, and heard about me from friends. He got the job, and after the first season, I was asked to fill the pro's position at a country club in Richmond, Virginia. Again, I recommended Oleg, who met the Reynolds family of Reynolds Aluminum products. They took a liking to him and his beautiful wife, appreciated his multilingual strengths, and offered him company training and a good job. A few years later, he became their representative for Europe and lives in Brussels.

Problems for My Parents

After I moved to Australia, I learned that the Communists had nationalized my parents' business and land in Prague for expansion. They imprisoned my father on the pretext that he helped me escape and hoarded meat products. The Communist regime could always find some reason to imprison dissidents or anyone they wanted out of sight. They tried to get my father to confess that he had money in Switzerland and that he had given the money to me, which was absolutely absurd. They kept him in prison for about three years until his health deteriorated to the extent that he was dying. They finally let him go, and one month later, he died in my mother's arms. For a long time afterward, I was haunted by the fact that I was unable to attend his funeral. My mother was able to survive for many years thanks to my father's foresight. He had never spirited money to Switzerland as accused, but instead of putting it in the bank, he bought gold coins whenever he could and hid them at the grave of my grandfather. My mother had enough coins to sell for many years to survive under the Communist regime. Whatever was left, she brought with her when she visited us in New York, and I have treasured them as souvenirs for my children.

Margie and I discovered that, except for the tennis activity and her good job, we did not like Australia. We missed European culture and the finer things in life that we had grown accustomed to in pre-war Europe. We could overcome our shock at being served spaghetti sandwiches, but the bias against outsiders was prominent, in contrast to the official welcoming policy. For a young country full of pioneering spirit, Australia was surprisingly unfriendly in the fifties to newcomers. We were called "bloody new Australians" regardless of whether we were European or American. It was very difficult to get a better job for us New Australians because local Australians got preference, regardless if we had better knowledge or education. I found it interesting that I didn't see any immigrants of Asian ethnicity in the 50th. I think this was attributable to the influence of the war in the Pacific, which was still in the mind of the people. Since that time, Australia has changed very much and kept the same progress with western countries when I have visited thirty years later.

Since I had a very good resume of working for the Americans in Germany and Margie had the same for the US Army, our immigration papers came in just a few weeks. We left for New York, via Europe. We sailed back under better circumstances than we had on the way in, though I confess that while the ocean was bumpy on the way to Australia, it was our marriage that was hitting rough waters on the way to what should have been the next great chapter in our young lives. There were no huge battles. We simply wanted different things out of life, and we respected each other enough to be honest about it. I wanted to have children.

Leaving Australia for the USA

We made our way back to Southampton, England, on the *SS Australia*, and a month later, after staying with Margie's sister in Brussels, I sailed alone to the United States on the *S.S. 1 USA*, making it in the record time of three and half days. Margie stayed for three months with her sister in Belgium, where her sister's husband owned a very successful frozen food and ice cream business called Artic, which later spread throughout Europe. While she was there, I looked for a job and accommodations in New York. It was as difficult to rent an apartment as it was in Sydney. I found one small room in Elmhurst Queens. We had to pay rent equivalent fourteen days of our salaries. She did join me later, though we eventually divorced, without bitterness. We have remained friends for life, even as we both remarried, and Margie became the godmother to my daughter, Andrea. I was happy for Margie, hoping that becoming an active and involved godmother helped fill a vacuum left by our dissolved marriage. I still admire her. She is a wonderful woman and her husband, Kurt, is very lucky. They live happily in retirement in Florida and occasionally entertain seniors in hospitals...Margie playing piano and Kurt singing (He used to be a professional opera singer).

The short voyage from Europe to America was filled with good moments. The night before we docked, I even won a dance contest in which partners had to hold a balloon between their heads, as I was dancing with an attractive college student from Washington. She asked me why I had escaped from the beautiful Czech Republic. I explained it to her, but I doubt that she understood it. As we approached New York Harbor, she and I stood at the railing on the top deck, staring at the emigrant's symbol of freedom, the Statue of Liberty—two people from very different worlds for whom the statue meant different things, but both of recognized its significance. With the Manhattan skyline ahead, I was elated—and scared. I had made it to New York at thirty years old, bearing an unfinished degree from Charles University that would do me no good, a thick accent, and absolutely no idea where I was headed next. Painful and joyous memories tumbled into one another— the simplicity of boyhood in pre-war Europe and the loss of that innocence in war. The atrocities, the refugee camps, the danger and fleeing, the cold, and the hunger had squeezed the youth right out of me. All of a sudden, just as I should have been feeling excited about a new life, I felt old and tired. Time and time again, I had barely escaped with my life or pleaded for others' lives to be spared. I did what I had to do, just like thousands of others. And I did it without shame. I traded illegal currency, played the black market, helped transport strangers across borders, and created homemade passports so refugees could flee or land jobs in new places. I had lived on three continents, and throughout, the one constant that kept me company on my adventures was symbolized by the wooden racket I held in my hands.

Chapter Four:
Not Enough Tennis
Clubs in New York

The past was past. I was in New York City, and once the initial fear and fatigue passed, it felt like every muscle in my body was alive. I began hunting for a job, and with every piece of sidewalk I pounded I wondered why a city like New York did not have more tennis clubs. The better-run private clubs that did exist, as I found out later, were so exclusive that you practically had to be a descendant of the *Mayflower* families to join. In Europe or Australia, in addition to the public courts, there were countless little tennis clubs available to anyone who could afford them, without needing ten letters of recommendation and a waiting list. Having played at some of them, I knew how they were managed, and I began thinking of starting my own enterprise in tennis or in other ventures. Through various jobs as a tennis pro at the River Club in New York City and another at the Rockaway Hunt Club in Lawrence, Long Island—I was constantly thinking about ways to improve my little income and quality of life. I would turn out to be what they call now an entrepreneur, but back then, I was just trying to figure out a way to get ahead.

We had left Australia just as tennis was coming into its own. I had the good fortune to play there and improved my game. In the United States in the late 1950s, tennis had hardly captured newspapers headlines. It was baseball country. But I was here and I was determined to look for opportunity in tennis field.

When we decided to leave Australia, I had written to my father's former lawyer in New York, Dr. Boruvka, whom I had already met at a DP camp in Ludwigsburg, to see if he could help get me a job as a teaching tennis pro in the States. It turned out that he knew someone who knew someone …

"You Want to Teach?" "Build Them Yourself."

I nearly jumped for joy when he said, "You have to go to see the manager of the New Rochelle Shore Club. My friend made an appointment for you. Hooray! I was on my way in America. I showed up the next morning eager to start—racket in hand, grin on my face—explaining that I was the new pro. A man whose ruddy complexion was evidently a result of the alcohol he breathed out with every syllable, said, "You want to teach?" And he showed me the place. "This used to be the tennis courts in 1930; you want to teach here, you have to build it yourself."

He pointed in the general direction of an area covered by grass and weeds over two feet high. Was there a court under there somewhere? Though there was—indeed, even a beautiful clubhouse—the immediate surroundings for what had once been tennis courts was just pasture. Any accidental brush with rusty chicken-wire fencing would require an immediate trip to an emergency room for a tetanus shot. It was a far cry from the small tennis clubs of my home country and worlds away from the new popularity that tennis had gained in Australia. Still, it was a start. They gave me two loads of red clay, a hand roller, and a roll of new chicken wire. For more than two weeks, I labored from four in the morning to nightfall, weeding and digging out the clay with pick and shovel, and on the fourteenth day, two courts were ready for play and I was ready for my new life. With every rivulet of sweat and aching muscle, I knew that finding lost tennis courts under mounds of neglect, beat going to night school, hands down. I had been thinking of attending Columbia University to turn my useless unfinished law degree into a useful law degree in America, but I changed my mind after consulting with a few of my friends and having dinner with my father's former lawyer from Czechoslovakia—the same Dr. Boruvka who had turned me onto the job at the New Rochelle Club. One day Dr. Boruvka invited Margie and me to his home in Brooklyn for dinner. It was an interesting dinner because his wife was a chef at a very well-known restaurant, the Viennese Lantern, which was visited very often by actress Lucille Ball, and the food she prepared was excellent. The only problem was that, with at least ten cats running around the table, some of their fur found its way into the food. But after displaced persons (DP) camps and some of our other less glamorous experiences, it was heavenly and only served to reinforce my desire to live well. I decided right then and there that I'd rather put in the hard work of restoring courts and have the pleasure of teaching others while playing the sport rather than sit in a class and maybe someday practice law.

Still, even after bringing tennis back to the New Rochelle Club, the ruddy Irish manager would not allow me to eat in the clubhouse. At lunchtime, I had to eat while sitting on the back stoop. But it did not take long for players to return to the club for tennis, and then I became a popular pro. By mid-summer, I was fully booked with children's classes, and we were running club tournaments. The club members threw a big party for me and asked me to return the next summer.

The following March, I entered a springtime professional teaching tournament at Boulevard Garden Tennis Club in Queens, which was run by a former German prisoner of war, George Harriy. I won the tournament and, as a result, was offered a position as an assistant pro to Bill Douglas at the River Club, where I would end up staying for thirteen winters, teaching on its two indoor courts. While I was moving up inch by inch in teaching, I was also looking at possible entrepreneurial opportunities. I believed the potential was there and that creating courts in New York where people could play would help the sport grow, provide recreation, and offer a means of at last making a living doing something I truly enjoyed.

River Club, New York

Being hired by River Club after winning professional teachers tournament in Queens

During my first week of teaching at the River Club, I was booked with a good player who wanted to improve his serve. After the lesson, we chatted a little, and I found out that he was born in Czechoslovakia and that his parents didn't trust the peace agreement—marked by Chamberlain's landing at a London airport with a sign that said "Peace Forever"—so they immigrated to England and later to the States. I immediately felt a bond with him because of our same country of origin. A few months later, during my lunchtime, I went skating one block away at the Town and Tennis Club, which had a skating rink on the roof of the garage building. I saw two little kids struggling on the ice. I tried to show them how to keep their balance. After a while, a young, beautiful lady came to me and thanked me, saying, "I am Angela Wyman, and these are my children, Freddy and Carol." What a coincidence—this was the wife of my pupil at the River Club, Frank Wyman. So started my lifelong friendship with the family, which later involved skiing, tennis, and parties, as well as Frank and his lovely wife, Angel, being the best man at my wedding to Annegret at the Plaza Hotel. Through him I met some of his social friends, including Donald Kendall. Don had just started his successful career with PepsiCo and became my second-oldest lifelong friend in America. Don has had a fascinating life. He told us many interesting stories about starting a Pepsi Cola business in Russia and drinking with Khrushchev. All three of us recently celebrated our ninetieth birthdays within a six-month period. I encountered many other famous personalities in the twelve-year period I was employed at the River Club. During the first few years,

I had a student who was a famous plastic surgeon, Dr. John Marquis Converse whose dream was to win the club championship. With my coaching, he succeeded and the world came around to Freddie Botur being recognized as the best teacher. It had some drawbacks by being all the time invited and since I was a non-drinker. One of the clients, the Wilhemsens put me on the spot; when at one of the dinners, there was a lady across the table and as was Norwegian custom, every time she picked up the glass I had to be polite, look at her eyes and drink it. Of course, after dinner when I stood up I don't know what happened but I fell under the table. It was part of my many lessons in the United States. Looking back, it was a different era in late fifties because of the postwar environment, and for me there were daily experiences regarding the American way of life. Every time I was booked with a pupil, it began another experience. I especially remember discovering that one of them was a "Rosie the Riveter," one of the first American women who volunteered to work in a factory to build war equipment. She and her family were my regular pupils.

C. V. Starr, Founder of A.I.U., Later A.I.G.

At both clubs—the River Club and Rockaway Hunting Club—I met people who became friends for life: Frank Wyman; Donald Kendall of PepsiCo; C. V. Starr, founder and 95-percent owner of American International Underwriters, which later became AIG; and many others. C. V. Starr would become one of the most powerful influences in my life, and I firmly believe that without him as a friend, my life experiences would not have been as rich as they were. We had our disagreements, including a major one over my second marriage—he felt that Annegret was too young for me and said so in slightly less-polite words—but overall, Starr, with whom I have traveled around the world as a tennis pro and friend, was one of the three persons whose presence, kindness, insight, and wisdom enriched my life.

Our friendship started during my first year at the River Club. I was sitting in the locker room for the pros, and I overheard a gentlemen's voice asking at the front desk if he could play every morning from eight to nine. Bill, the head pro, said, "I don't come before ten." Upon hearing this, I stepped out and told the gentleman, "I will play at any time you want." That's how I met C. V. Starr, and that's when my real-life American university education started. I learned by listening to conversations among his friends or businessmen at the dinner parties to which he invited my first wife Margie and me. Starr had a limited number of close friends whom he invited to parties. Jim and Isabella Perkins (Jim was a lawyer for Paramount Pictures) were his favorites, and Madame Garnet of the Madame Garnet Fashion House, which he supported, was his protégé and good friend.

One of the highlights was the invitation to the opening of Madame Butterfly at the old New York Opera house. C.V. Starr financed the opening of the new production of Madame Butterfly, which was his favorite opera. It must have been something in his past living in the Far East that he had created a passion for it.

Starr considered me to be a good tennis pro, but after a few days he realized that I could be good company when he was under stress. Playing tennis allowed him to release tension and kept his mind off of his marital troubles. After his wife, Mary, had left him and lived in Paris. He came almost every day after making sure I had an open time that day. He started to improve after a few months and began to really like the game, so he decided to build two grass courts on the Brewster estate in Westchester, called "Morfar". He started to invite Margie and me to join him on the weekends where we met many interesting guests during the period of few years. At one point, he considered building one indoor tennis court, which my friend Z. Capek designed, but he decided on a far bigger project—building his own golf course on which he could put all his entire sculpture collection.

Starr always included us when he had dinners with his friends. Very often, artists like Dong Kingman, top tennis players like Margaret Smith, or the world's best skiers, like Buddy Werner (who died in an avalanche) and Toni Sailer attended. I will never forget when the architect I. M. Pei visited, which extended my list of famous people I have met.

Starr was very often visited by the chairman of his board, Gordon Tweedy; his wife, Mary; and their three daughters. Starr was very fond of them and felt them to be a part of his family, especially after his wife left him. He felt lonely but was still in love with her and always thought that she would return to him. He even made a substantial monetary arrangement to enable her to live comfortably in Paris, but his dream of her return never came true.

Also, I have to mention that he was enthusiastic skier before he started playing tennis and was also an investor in ski developing lifts in St. Anton, Austria, and in Stowe, Vermont, at The Lodge. Since I was also a good skier, Starr often invited me to join him on a trip to Stowe on his small, old plane, piloted by war veteran Captain Watson. Starr sponsored many foreign students from the Middle and Far East, and some of them came on certain weekends. One of his favorite students was Chiharu Igaya, whom he sponsored at Dartmouth College, and another student protégé was Richard Liesching. He also sponsored some students from Far Eastern Countries, but I cannot recall their names.

All of the new surroundings, exposed the different cultures way of life, and the different cultures made for an interesting period of my life. It seems that interesting moments occurred daily in teaching tennis, which also involved listening to people's personal problems and sympathizing with them. I think this was part of why I was well liked and had good and steady clientele and many of them became good friends.

Chiharu Igaya, while still studying, won a silver medal in skiing for Japan in the Olympic Games. After a while, one loses track of many friends or acquaintances, and only on some occasions or by accident can they connect again. On my honeymoon with Annegret, we stopped in Tokyo and had lunch with Igaya. Years later, Starr told me that after Igaya completed his studies and employment at AIU, he became the head of Starr's successful insurance company in Tokyo and became very friendly with Japanese Prince Akihito, with whom he played tennis occasionally. After the prince's father died, he became Emperor Akihito.

Whenever Starr needed to entertain anybody with a few tennis matches or in a social situation, he would take me on the trips as his companion. Together, I went to Hong Kong, Tokyo, Beirut, Paris, and other places in Europe. On those trips, I met many of his Chinese friends, like K.K. Tse (who also built his summer house in Brewster next to C.V. Starr's estate. K.K. was one of the few people who knew how close I was to C.V. Starr and invited me for lunches very often at his AIG office or his home in Brewster, after Starr died, this continued until his death in 1998. K.K. was one of the finest of all Starr's friends and associates. I am sorry that I wasn't able to keep in contact with the family because of my health problems at the time.), Tai Tchung, Tony Liang, and many others whose names I could not pronounce or spell. (But I have their pictures.) Margie and I were frequently his guests, staying with him at the main house at Morfar in Westchester or his mansion in Hong Kong, Stowe, or St. Anton—wherever we were invited. Most of his homes had Chinese staff, and his favorite chef was Ling.

Entrepreneurship was part of the American dream, and I was on American soil. People liked my accent and somehow found my background as a refugee who escaped communism life interesting, soon members of both clubs began to invite me and my wife regularly to dinners, the theatre, and many social events. Starr really was my tutor.

On one occasion, he was traveling to a board meeting in Hong Kong and asked if I would like to attend. I told him that I thought it would be a great experience. Starr introduced me at the meeting as his friend and asked the servant to pull up an extra chair for me next to him. It was a fascinating experience for me, observing the process of debates between the officers of the corporation and hearing Starr's questions. It was interesting to see his reaction, at one point, he got up and said, "Gentleman, when you agree and are ready, I'll be back in three months." (It seemed to me that he had made his decision already before the meeting.) During our friendship, I was offered an opportunity to train at AIU (American

International Underwriters) and start a job, but I told him that I was not the kind of man who could sit for hours between four walls. He said, "It's your decision."

In the early seventies, Starr had to decide whom to appoint as his successor at AIU. He mentioned two of his best officers, G. Tweedy and W. Youngman. These two men, he confided to me one day after lunch, were getting older and didn't have the drive to run and enlarge the company. "So I have been looking for somebody outside," he said. "I found a young Jewish boy from Chicago whom I will interview this afternoon."

First Attempt to Build a Tennis Club in N.Y.

In 1958, while I was teaching at the River Club at the age of 36 full of energy, I saw my first opportunity. I could lease the roof of the Miles Shoe Building on the west side of Manhattan. I had the backing of about twenty River Club members, including Laurence Rockefeller, who was my regular pupil. Each promised to invest a thousand dollars in my venture. The prospect held promise, had architect draw plans and I was all set to go until a few months after we presented our plans, when the owners suddenly informed me that the Lincoln Center was going to be built across the street. It was my first introduction to the real estate that would dominate my life for the next four decades. I was not able to secure a lease because the owners decided that the property was too valuable for tennis courts if the Lincoln Center was going up across the way. But I had learned my first lesson in the real estate business.

With the Miles Shoe Building off limits, I began seeking to start a club on the roof of the New York Coliseum. That, too, looked promising until the owners objected because they feared that tennis would distract employees who could look out of the windows of the building that rose thirty stories above the Coliseum. Later, I also lost a bid to build my tennis club on the roof of the Eastern Airline terminal on Thirty-Sixth Street to a higher bidder.

Meanwhile, I continued to teach tennis on the two indoor courts at the famed River Club on Fifty-Second Street and East River in the winter and at the Rockaway Hunting Club in the summer. Three years after I started at the River Club, the pro, Bill Douglas, decided to retire. He had made a small fortune investing in oil exploration on the advice of one of the members. I was happy for his good fortune, and I was even happier that he suggested me as his replacement. I started to order tennis rackets from Wilson Sporting Goods Company with my own signature just like some more famous players. A fellow from a village in Czechoslovakia with a name that members could not even pronounce now had a title they could easily say: head pro. It was a long way from being relegated to eating a sandwich on the back stoop at courts I had dug out at New Rochelle.

Rockaway Hunting Club, 1887

After my second year as the pro at the River Club, member, a well- known neurosurgeon named T. I. Hoen who enjoyed hitting with me as often as his time would allow, said "Freddie, we are looking for a new pro for the summer at the Rockaway Hunting Club. You would be the right guy to replace US pro championship 1945 winner Welby van Horn. I hope you don't mind, but I have entered your name as a candidate, and I think I have enough friends to get you in."

It seemed like everywhere I turned, there were business people and professionals like Dr. Hoen who went on to be one of the most published neurosurgeons ever, who were willing to go out of their way to help me professionally. Nobody in the eastern Communist countries would believe my start in free, democratic America or how well the Americans treated me, with respect and freedom of expression. They would have called me a liar if I had tried to explain it to them. Things in America happened to me like they would in a fairy tale.

I asked Dr. Hoen if he could show me the courts. He drove me out on a Saturday, and I was stunned. I was looking at the most perfectly maintained sixteen grass courts, eight red clay courts, and a beautiful golf club overlooking the bay. It was like a movie set. I tried to think of another word, but all I could say was, "Beautiful." I had never seen grass so green or courts so well maintained, except in Sydney, or a whole package like that, and it was being offered to me.

I was told that the club members had talked of getting Fred Perry, who was number one in the world, to be the pro, but they wanted a real teaching pro, not just a famous name attached to the club. So an unknown Czech player named Freddie got the job.

After only a few years in the States, I was able to put a three-thousand-dollar down payment on a small house in Cedarhurst that I bought for fifteen thousand dollars. In the summer, I didn't have to drive to work, and was no longer paying rent. In the winter, I drove every day to the city, where parking was difficult, and I got lot of parking tickets. But I had landed jobs at the two best private tennis clubs in New York. I also joined the Professional Tennis Teachers Association, and before I knew it, I was president for one year. I think because of being pro at prestigious two clubs. Professional standards were so simple in those days. Anybody who wanted to become a teaching pro was asked three questions: How long have you been playing tennis? Are you single or married? Do you have fifty dollars to pay for the enrollment? That sums up the purely run organization of tennis teachers in the late 1950s. After being recommended for the position at the Rockaway Hunting Club and interviewed by Donald Grant, one of the founders of the New York Mets, I got the job at one of the oldest country clubs in the United States. In 1887, it was a club with a history of old American families, the club had fox hunting and horse racing, and membership was exclusive and limited. Within a week, I was booked every day for the rest of the season, the majority of my pupils being children. Again, I was amazed. Annegret and I were treated just like members of the club and given membership at the beach club. After I started my own clubs, (Tennis Inc. and West Park Racket Club, Tennis 59, and Cedarhurst T.C) I recommended my RHC assistant, Stan Nielsen (Nepomucky in Czech) as my replacement for both of my positions. I became a full member of the RHC and bought a house next to the tennis courts.

In 2012 I was honored, by the Rockaway Hunting Club, they presented me with a plaque, which was installed on court number seven, for my service to the community and mainly to the children I had taught. It was a surprise party for me, which had over a hundred members in attendance, "many of them are already grandfathers and grandmothers". It was really a great surprise.

My junior team going to Richmond, to play Richmond Country Club.

Back home in New York, before our worlds expanded, I was still coaching. During my twelve years at the Rockaway Hunting Club I took the junior players from the club to friendly team matches in California, Canada, and Virginia, as well as to many local team matches. It was exciting for the juniors and me to travel and visit and meet other clubs. Our juniors played Vic Braden team and Nick Bollettieri teams when they still were unknown. On many of the overnight tennis trips, my wife Annegret was a helpful guardian, making sure that there was no misbehavior.

Surprised by Sergeant Zeese

At one of the organization's meetings, there were about eight applicants asking for certification as tennis teaching professionals. I looked up at one point and could not believe my eyes. There was my old friend from Bremerhaven, Sergeant Herb Zeese, the man who had given me a job while I was stuck waiting for the ship. We started hugging and clasping hands and reminiscing. He told me that he had retired from the army and was looking for a job, and he fell in love with tennis after I gave him the start. I gave him an opportunity to be my assistant so he could keep in shape, and about six months later, a member of the River Club with whom I played tennis, Clarence Dauphinot, asked me if I could recommend somebody for a position as a teaching pro at the Lyford Cay Club in The Bahamas. I replied that I could recommend a very charming, likable, and dependable tennis teacher who had just retired from the Army. I was happy when Herb was accepted, and he stayed for at least ten years. Then, the Bahamas became independent, and he had to be replaced by a Bahamian pro. He returned to the States and soon mentioned to me that a piece of land was for sale in Huntington, Long Island, where he lived and owned a house. He was able to get a mortgage and built a very nice tennis club, the Huntington Racquet Club, naming me as vice president. His great personality and affable way made him immensely popular, and I am touched that even many years after his death, his daughter, Bonnie Dorland, to whom I became a godfather continues to keep in touch and has never once forgotten my birthday. She is a success in the financial services industry in New York City and is married with two children. The world is filled with coincidences that change lives, and I was blessed to have encountered so many at such a young age.

Bobby Riggs

It was one Sunday at the Rockaway Hunting Club that I had one of the most humorous and eye-opening experiences of my life, an exhibition match with Bobby Riggs. I got a phone call from the manager of the nearby Woodmere Country Club, asking me to step in as a fourth in an exhibition match with Riggs at noon. They'd pay me two hundred dollars for it. That was huge money for me in those days, when I was earning eight dollars per lesson. I had to cancel a few lessons and went to the club; where on the small tribune sat a few hundred spectators waiting for the exhibition. When we started to play, I tried my best in the first set, but we were losing 4–3. I was frustrated because Riggs looked like a walking duck, and I was trying my best. Finally, he said, "Only hit the balls that come to you," and we won the first set. A similar thing happened in the second set; when we were behind and changing sides, he spoke a few words to about five fans who were sitting next to the tennis court. I did not realize then that every time we changed sides, he was betting with those five guys. I was new to the country and more than a little naive about betting in tennis. After we won, he handed me three hundred dollars and said, "This is your share of my winnings, partner." In years to come, we played on a few occasions. Riggs, who was as well known for his love of betting as for his dedication to the game, was once quoted as saying, "If I can't play for big money, I play for a little money. And if I can't play for a little money, I stay in bed that day." In fact, he was really a wonderful tennis partner and, in his own way, did a lot to generate interest in tennis among the general public. In the famous 1973 Battle of the Sexes match, he lost three straight sets to Billie Jean King after boasting of his male superiority. I was saddened to learn of his death in 1995.

C.V Starr Interviewing for Future Chairmanship

At two o'clock that Saturday afternoon, Starr and I were sitting under a huge tree not far from the house when Ling, Starr's favorite cook, came and said that there was a young couple there to see him. Starr said to send for them. When they joined us, they were introduced as Mr. and Mrs. Greenberg. I shook hands with them and left, knowing Starr wanted to be alone to interview them. About an hour later, he told me, "He is my man." Hank Greenberg was hired, and I was the first person that day to know it.

When C. V. Starr died a few years later of emphysema, Hank Greenberg took over a company valued at approximately $700 million. Greenberg restructured it and renamed it AIG. Today, its value is more than $100 billion—making it the most successful insurance company in the world, according to the *Wall Street Journal*. Starr's Foundation made many scholarships for young people especially from Middle and Far eastern countries. Ling his cook ended up sending his children to college, and one of his

Playing in Hong Kong with C.V. Starr.

C.V. Starr

Mr and Mrs Tweedy, Margie and myself, having dinner with C.V. Starr.

daughters became a science engineer in the United States. Ling has since died, but his widow is still around and lives in Queens next door to my friend Mr. Capek.

One day, while I was playing tennis at Tennisport, one of my members, Mr. Sullivan, told me that his friend, a writer named Walter Guzzardi, had been assigned to write a company-sponsored biography of C. V. Starr. Guzzardi was interested in what I knew about him.

In January 1996, Guzzardi and Sullivan came to visit me at the club and gave me the first draft of Starr's biography, entitled *"Taking Risks."* Then, about six months later, I heard that the contract had been canceled. My personal opinion is that somebody in the company had not liked what Guzzardi had written so far. He gave me a copy of his first seventy-seven pages of his writing.

Starr was born in Fort Bragg, California, in 1892. He arrived in Shanghai in 1919 with empty pockets, no friends, and no business oppurtunities. The Chinese had never heard of him, but by the time he died, he was wealthy and enjoyed a large circle of influential associates who were well known around the world. Starr left most of his money to educational and medical foundations. One of Starr's closest associates, Mr. Freedman, had his summer home next to Starr's in Brewster, New York. Freedman had once been stationed in Tokyo, where he invited Starr and me to join him for Thanksgiving dinner when Starr had stopped in Tokyo for a few days after a trip to Hong Kong. It was my first Thanksgiving dinner, and that delicious dish of sweet potatoes with marshmallows was not known in my old country, but soon became my favorite dish. A few months after Starr past away, Mr. Greenberg took a few tennis lessons from me at the Tennis Inc. Armory at Thirty-Fourth Street and Park Avenue. He or his secretary usually booked his appointment the day before, but one day he walked into my club at the armory and asked for a lesson. That day, unfortunately, I was booked all day and told him I could not cancel the lessons. He got very upset and said, "For Starr, you would cancel one." I answered, "But you are not Mr. Starr." (I didn't have with him close personal contact, like I had with Starr for so many years.) He felt offended, left, and never called for an appointment again. Years later, we met socially, and he was friendly. We exchanged a few polite words.

The beginning of a new era of metal racquets.

Introduction of Metal Racquets

Maybe it was my first wife, Margie, with her language skills and charm, or my second wife, Annegret, with her spirit, kindness, and blonde beauty, that people really liked, but whatever it was, during both marriages, I found myself the recipient of many invitations and being engaged in a very active social life that I never would have dreamed of before moving to New York. It helped, too, that the occasional newspaper gossip touted me with some title that made me chuckle, but that kept my name alive far longer than I thought it deserved to be.

A 1977 *New York Times* story that ran after I won the eastern division singles and doubles ages 45 and 55 same year dubbed me "the new hero of the senior circuit." Another article discussed the alloy tennis racquet I helped to promote with Walter Montenegro, owner of Cragin-Simplex Company. The racquet did not enjoy the same longevity. There were basic flaws with the alloy that was available then. It made me think about how far sport equipment has come using new lighter materials.

Wilson introduced the first metal racket, the T2000, in 1967, and Jimmy Connors was quick to use it. Since then, nearly every combination of materials has been introduced: ceramic, fiberglass, boron, titanium, Kevlar, and graphite. Rackets weigh a lot less than they used to, and there are fewer cases of tennis elbow. Balls are now bright yellow instead of hard-to-see white. But for all the changes to scheduling and prize money, metal racquets, and their quality and color of the balls, did not change the mentality of the game to win.

What has changed very much over the years is the horrendous amount of sponsor's money. It gives incentive for children from relatively poor neighborhoods, who practice hitting balls against the wall to find success later in the game. It's for the adults who just need a break from stress, for doctors and politicians and students of all ages. Tennis is an equalizer where those with talent are free to compete.

Invitations and Challenges

As head pro at the River Club, which in the 50th was one of the most exclusive social club in America with two indoor tennis courts. The membership listed most powerful people in banking and government people. I was often invited to play at different clubs or events, sometimes to fill a corporate slot. It was as close to being a celebrity as I would get in those days, but I didn't mind because it paid much more than individual lessons, just as the Bobby Riggs exhibition match with betting benefits did. I never lost sight of how much I enjoyed tennis. It was fun—unadulterated, great fun. I think my happiness toward playing showed. I tried not to dwell on the shame my father had tried to instill in me when he failed to understand how much the game meant to me or how natural I felt on the court. In his day, playing tennis for money was like being a waiter. He thought an education in business administration and law would cure my desire to spend so much of my life with a racket in my hand and my eye on the ball. I regret that father didn't live long enough to see was how I managed to take something I loved—healthy, wholesome, and enriching tennis—and turn it into a successful business.

In the early days of my career in America, I appreciated the invitations to fill in for someone or to hit on a private court. One of those invitations that came regularly was from Percy Uris, at the time the most successful builder of office buildings in Manhattan. His own residence was a mansion with a private tennis court about an hour away, in Manhasset on Long Island. Uris wanted to play occasionally on the weekends. He set the rules: I was to play my whole doubles court while I had to hit it to him so he could reach the ball. If it was a little out of his reach, it was his point. The bet was a hundred dollars per set, and my lessons were ten dollars per hour. It was hard work, but Uris was elderly, so I understood the handicap I was giving him. The money was welcome, and I made the games very close to keep him happy.

Most unique and luxurious indoor at W. Burden's playhouse. The court is packed sand, the walls are covered with growing ivy, with a retractable roof, built in the 20s. The only court like that in America at the time.

Life is Worth Living

One other fascinating person whom I used to play twice a week in the wintertime at the River Club was His Excellency Bishop Fulton Sheen. He was a close friend of the Polish pope and had every popular television program: "*Life is worth living*" that aired twice a week; you can still occasionally see re-runs on some local Midwest stations. He mixed his program, making it half religious and half anti-communist. Since I was a refugee from the communist regime, the bishop liked our after-game discussions about the current Communist regime and why I had to flee from it. He was very friendly, and I attended his sermons in the private chapel a few times at his invitation. Because of his TV programs and political views, he was denied the opportunity to become a cardinal. After he passed away I was asked to serve as a member of the board of the Fulton Sheen Foundation.

Bishop Fulton Sheen.

I also played a few times with the general manager of the Waldorf-Astoria, a Mr. Bing, who was a guest of one of the members. He was a very enthusiastic player. Since Margie was looking for a job, I asked Mr. Bing if there would be one available at the hotel. "Send her to me," he said. We went to his office and found ten other people waiting for job interviews. Mr. Bing's secretary came out of the office and said, "Mr. Botur, come in—just you." Mr. Bing's office was huge. I had never seen one like it. It was complete with lots of books and paintings.

"Sit down, Freddie," and then we had a small talk and he asked me about my wife and what time we were going to play next day, then he said stay and watch until your wife turn comes. Several people came in carrying their portfolios, many of them from other hotels or hotel schools. Mr. Bing was very brief. He always said, "Thank you. We will let you know."

One man walked in, and as he was walking toward Mr. Bing's desk, he bent over to pick up a tiny piece of paper lying on the floor about eight feet in front of the desk. Without looking at his resume, Bing asked him a few questions and said, "You're hired." He later told me that he had put the piece of paper there on purpose to test the applicants' powers of observation. No school will teach things like that.

Then he interviewed Margie, and she got the job. Within six months, she was appointed as manager of the cafeteria. A year later, she was offered a managerial job with Marriot Hotels to run a small resort in Puerto Rico. She accepted, and I started the mutual and friendly divorce proceedings.

Lesson from Rolls Roycing with Vanderbilt

A few months after working at the River Club and getting acquainted with the way of life and social customs in New York City, I didn't expect the unusual pupil who one day came in. The club secretary, Ruth Unver, booked me with a Mr. Vanderbilt. I was new in the country, and I did not know who he was. I had somehow heard or read his name somewhere, but it didn't mean much to me—just another Social Register pupil. What I did know was that the River Club had very strict rules about dressing code only in white, and here came a tall, skinny elderly gentleman in a dingy white shirt with a hole in it, gray pants, and tennis shoes that had to have been at least ten years old. After about fifteen minutes of playing, he suggested that we take a break. He proceeded to talk about a World Series or other major sport. I did not have any idea what he was talking about, so I only nodded and said, "Yes, sir." Before another twenty minutes of hitting the ball, he invited me to go for a walk with him on the street. Since I was paid by the hour, it did not matter to me if I was walking or playing. That said, it was a rather unusual way for me to finish a tennis lesson. We walked from the club to First Avenue, and then we went up Fifty-Sixth Street and turned right, talking about the baseball game of the night before. "Yes, sir," I said and then Mr. Vanderbilt decided that we should head back. He moved his arm out and motioned with his finger. A uniformed chauffeur pulled up in a Rolls Royce, and we were driven back to the club. I had no idea that there had been a limousine following us while we walked toward the bridge. That was one of the strangest tennis lessons of my life. From then on, Mr. Vanderbilt usually booked for two hours. For the last half hour, his wife would come down from River House, where they lived, and finish the lesson. She was not able to take more than half an hour since she was not athletically strong enough, but she did get a little exercise.

From the beginning of my job at the Rockaway Hunting Club, Margie worked with me as an assistant, giving some lessons to the children and taking care of the tennis shop there. I had already opened the Tennis Inc. facility at Thirty-Fourth Street and Park Avenue, and I felt weak, overworked, and stressed, with such bad back pain that I could hardly walk. I was sent to St. Luke's Hospital, where one of the first members of Tennis Inc., Dr. Kittredge, handled the case personally and recommended surgery. While I appreciated his attention and concern and knew that St. Luke's was a top-notch facility, I was worried about undergoing the operation. Back surgery in the 1960s was very risky, but there was no getting around it, I was told. I had tests done in the hospital the day before shortly before the operation was scheduled. James Donovan, a good friend and member of the River Club, came to visit (His daughter, Christina, became one of the first members of the West Park Racquet Club). He brought a friend who had been a British Royal Air Force pilot during the war. The two men had been stationed together at the same US military unit during the Chiang Kai-shek era in China and had known friends and soldiers who had undergone similar operations in the last few years. They urged me to cancel the surgery and leave the hospital. The RAF pilot showed me specific exercises, by pressing my arms and stomach and buttocks at the same time to do. I felt a slight improvement. I was so scared about the operation, that I put my clothes on when nobody was around and ran away from the hospital the day before my surgery, embarrassing Dr. Kittredge. I continued the exercises, and within three weeks I was back on the tennis court. And to this day, whenever I feel even a little pain, I go back to the exercises I learned much by accident from a friend of a friend. I thanked him for saving me from what could have been a disastrous mistake. I was saved from the scalpel, but I still had a long way to go to make my plans for dotting the New York landscape with affordable tennis clubs where everyone could enjoy the sport. I was coming up in the world of professionals, landing jobs in two of the best clubs, traveling as a private pro around the world, and playing on private courts at posh residences. But the dream of entrepreneurship, in the sport I had first encountered on a vacation with my mother at the age of twelve, was still fifty years away.

Tennis Inc., in the Armory, 1965-1968, and Sponsoring Pro Tournaments

The Armory at 34th Street and Park Avenue, where the Pros played this year, has reasonable lighting but a very rough wooden floor. The sponsors of the tournament laid down an additional wooden floor, then covered it with a huge strip of rubber. The surface was approximately as slow as clay and the bounce relatively true. This is Saturday night at the Armory, with Andres Gimeno (far court) walking over to serve to Rod Laver. Up above one can see the five flags of the five countries that were represented, and to the right additional flags were draped over the second balcony and the boxes. Photo, P. W. Trostorff.

My first Pro adventure in New York (picture of Laver vs. Bucholz)

One day, in 1965, my real estate luck changed. I got a phone call from one of the old-timers who had run the armory in the Bronx in the 1940s. He asked me if I would be interested in opening a tennis club at the armory in Manhattan at Thirty-Fourth Street and Park Avenue. He said he would give me all the necessary information if I would let him run it. I had managed to save up a few thousand dollars, and I agreed. C. V. Starr rose to the occasion by supporting me and getting his AIU lawyer, Frank Starett, to prepare the legal documents. My first tennis club, named Tennis Inc., officially opened with five indoor courts in 1965. I had been lucky to win the bid against Gene Scott, a well-known tennis player who later became a popular tournament commentator and publisher of *Tennis Weekly* magazine. I think my partner had better connections.

My First Tennis Enterprise
Tennis Inc. Opening Day and Being Fired

By the time the club opened, I already had two hundred members signed up at two hundred dollars per person. My costs were low: I paid twenty dollars per day to the state, which included heat and electricity. It seemed like a great business deal. There were a few drawbacks; there were no facilities, except the army-style showers and toilets located on the upper level, so we had to create facilities, adding expense. The

My favourite pupil, Dina Merill.

lighting was miserable, and redoing it became another expensive improvement. Plus we had to move out completely when the National Guard unit came in for exercises, complete with their trucks and mortars, about twice a week. But we resolved to work our schedule around theirs.

Nevertheless, on opening day, I had a picture taken with Dina Merrill, the daughter of Marjorie Merriweather Post. Dina, who owned the Maro Lago (now the residence of President Donald Trump) would go on to become a major film star, at that time was married to a great sportsman Stan Rumbough, and the couple's three children had been my pupils at the River Club. For the picture, Dina and I stood in front of the armory under the green canopy with a sign that said "Tennis Inc." One of the major New York dailies, either the *New York Times* or the *Wall Street Journal*—I cannot remember which one—ran an article with our picture. Following the photo session, Dina and I went inside to hit a few balls. To my horror, I found that the balls were getting covered with splinters. The floor at the armory was rotten wood! That was the end of the opening.

For a moment, I was at a loss for what to do. I had not seen my manager that morning, but when I came back at noon I discovered him drunk. I learned from others that he had been drunk every day. I paid him a sufficient amount of money for introducing me to the place and let him go.

It was raining the day I let him go, and on the way out of the armory, I was so shaken that I tripped over the rubber matting at the exit door, a fortuitous misstep. The other side of the wet rubber matting, which flipped over when I tripped, was lined with canvas. I said to myself, this is a solution for the courts. I called the US Rubber Company, which made the matting, and asked if they would send me seventy rolls that were sixty feet long by six feet wide. They had them in stock. Then, I thought, *how can I seal these rolls together to make this a portable tennis court?* I was young and full of energy; nothing was going to stop me.

I called up my friend Zdenek Capek, the man who had once been my roommate at Mrs. Heim's in Frankfurt and who had built a mini car fifty years ahead of its time. Capek had become a well-known engineer with a highly successful company in Queens,

International Development Engineers, which was manufacturing noiseless apparatuses for the US Navy. I asked him to look into what kind of glue or epoxy would bind the matting to form the four pieces for one court. It took him less than a day to find the epoxy that did the job. Two days later, US Rubber delivered the rolls of rubber matting. With Capek's help and a system to fuse the matting, twenty students from Columbia University worked three nights to glue the rolls together. We worked as quickly as possible.

*My invention of portable Tennis Courts which I
sold the "know how" to US Rubber Corp*

Because the National Guard used the armory for exercises on certain days, there were many days that we could not play a full day, and some days we could not play at all. I was afraid that if we left the mats on the floor, they would be destroyed by the jeeps and trucks. But the problem, we realized as soon as we finished the first mat, was that each was so heavy that it took several men just to roll one quarter of it onto and off of the court. Once again, I turned to Zdenek. He designed and built tubing that made it easier to roll the mats on and off. In the end, the portable mats were so successful that the US Rubber Company wanted to know how I had done it. I sold the know-how to them for ten thousand dollars, which paid for my initial expenses for opening the armory, which opened only 14 days late. US Rubber then invested a few hundred thousand dollars in portable tennis courts and began marketing them in all the tennis magazines. They got inquiries, but because the company was so big and bureaucratic, and because they tried to improve the product, they were slow in delivering. Their delay would cost them.

In the meantime, after seeing my success in the armory, a tennis player named Sidney Wood found that he could make portable tennis courts with synthetic grass instead of rubber. He beat US Rubber to the market, and US Rubber gave the product up.

About a month after I opened Tennis Inc., the chairman of the River Club, Arthur McPherson, came to the tennis desk where we arranged games and told me that my services were no longer required. My life was just coming together and, to my horror, I was being fired.

"Here is a check for one month's advance salary," he said. "There were some phone calls through the switchboard to you from your other club, which I hear you own, and that is a conflict of interest. You can leave tomorrow because we do not want our professionals to be associated with a club which is not up to our standards." Over the next few days, he received dozens of letters in my favor, but nothing could change his mind. My assistant, Al Doyle, replaced me.

Although I didn't realize it right away, getting fired was a blessing in disguise. Suddenly, I had to take care of my own club or else. I had to be at the armory twelve hours a day to monitor, improve, and grow the business. To supplement the start-up income from the armory, and before that the income from teaching at the River Club, I was still teaching in the summer at the Rockaway Hunting Club, whose board of directors had no objection to my other tennis business. In addition, I had a good assistant, Stan Nielsen (Nepomucky), a former national Czech hockey player who later became the new pro at the River Club.

Jack Kramer: "Freddie, nobody wants us." 1966

In 1966, when I had the Thirty-Fourth Street armory, Jack Kramer, the world famous player and promoter, approached me and asked me to put up fifteen thousand dollars in prize money for a tournament he wanted to organize early in 1967. He had eight professionals set to go but no place to host the tournament and no prize money to offer.

"Freddie, nobody wants us," Kramer said. "Madison Square Garden does not want us. White Plains does not want us."

I could not believe that a great and famous player like Jack Kramer was coming to me, an unknown immigrant, to ask if I would be interested in promoting the tournament. I thought about it for a little less than a minute, knew instantly that we could accommodate nearly four thousand people in the armory, and determined that I would make it happen. A few days later, I received a letter of confirmation from his manager, Mr. Wills. The players he was proposing were the most famous names in the game. We just needed to come up with the prize money. Since we did not have anyone who could sponsor us, I put up five thousand dollars myself and asked two of my friends—Lieberman, vice president of a gas company, and Zdenek Capek, the engineer friend who helped me design the roll-up mats for the armory—to invest five thousand dollars each.

I can still name the singles draw from the top down: Rod Laver, Fred Stolle, Dennis Ralston, Butch Buchholz, Pancho Gonzalez, Pierre Barthes, Mike Davis, Andres Gimeno, Pancho Segura, and Cliff Drysdale. No one was willing to underwrite the event. Our close friends tried to help us promote it, distributing the leaflets on the streets. The media ignored us except for praising the matches the day after the finals.

The finals, in which Gonzalez beat Laver, lasted five and a half hours. New York *Times* reporter Allison Danzig called it one of the longest games he had ever seen. The publicity from him, the tennis guru, on the whole sports page of the New York *Times* came, unfortunately, too late.

At one point during the tournament, I wanted to know how good I was against the world's number one tennis player, Pancho Gonzalez. He was tall, he had film-star good looks, and women were just crazy about him. I asked him what handicap he would give me if we played one set for a hundred dollars, a lot of money for me in 1967.

We played. He gave me five games and 30–love in each. I stretched, warmed up, shook loose, psyched up, and powered up, but nothing helped. I didn't return his serves and missed his forehands, backhands, and cross courts—everything and never won a game. Experiencing the difference between a mediocre player and a real champion was a stunning eye-opener, well worth the hundred dollars to learn the lesson, although Pancho had tried to refuse to accept it. "Freddie, I do not want to take your money," he said kindly after whipping my pride.

Presenting trophy of the tournament to Rod Laver

Gonzales' classic backhand volley

Last Pro Tournaments before 1968 Wimbledon Open

Rod Laver, challenging me to beer after tournament.

Unfortunately, the tournament was as much a financial disaster for us as the set against Pancho had been a personal one for me. The finals were held on a Sunday afternoon and conflicted with other sports events that day. The trophy and prize were presented by Ed Sullivan, the famous TV personality.

For this event we had printed four thousand tickets, sold three hundred, and had to give away two hundred to people who helped us—ball boys, umpires, etc. In addition to putting up the prize money, I had paid all the expenses for the players, including airfare and hotels.

They still didn't have a sponsor, though, and asked me to run the tournament again the following year, this time with Mal Anderson, Roy Emerson, Barry McKay, Rosewall, Fred Stolle, Pancho Segura, and Dennis Rolston.

Humble beginnings often turn out to have significant endings, and I am humbled and proud to know that those early days spent helping the stranded the touring pros, who a year later become an Open amateur and competed in professional championships in Wimbledon. In the history of tennis, previous amateurs tournaments were attended only by invitation, and the Open is considered routine now.

Winning Seniors Eastern Grass Court Championships and Entering Wimbledon, 45 Seniors Doubles, 1968

For every dark cloud, a ray of sunshine follows, and one of those rays came in 1977 when I entered and won same year the Eastern Grass Court Championship, at the age of 55 divisions for singles and doubles with Tony Vincent and also 45 singles.

My first opportunity was at the Open Wimbledon in 1968, I intended to enter the 45-and-over senior doubles tournament with Frank Parker, whom I had met a few times and had practice on RHC courts on grass, just like many other top tennis players when they didn't have the opportunity to practice one the Forest Hills courts. (Forest Hills Club didn't want to damage the grass courts before the tournament.) Bill Talbert appreciated it and for that he allocated a corner box for me at Forest Hills stadium. At the last minute, Parker withdrew to return to the United States to attend to his wife, who was seriously ill. Annegret, who had accompanied me, was disappointed, but luckily Sir James Harvie-Watt, committee chairman, asked if I could do him a favor and play with Herman Schaefer instead of looking for a replacement. He said that Schaefer was a V.P. of PepsiCo, responsible for sponsoring the tournament. "Why not?" I answered, since I didn't have anybody else to replace.

William Talbert, who appreciated the use of grass courts at RHC for top players during the US Open

Even though Schaefer was not a tournament player, we had a wonderful time playing. I felt very excited. Every time I left the clubhouse, I was met by a group of tennis fans asking for autographs and, now when I watch TV matches, I have a feeling of satisfaction that "I was there." Annegret also enjoyed her time at Wimbledon and the excitement.

Despite our success in renovating the armory facility, hosting tennis tournaments, and creating a place where people could play tennis year-round inexpensively, the armory and my first tennis club were doomed. Its appointment with a wrecking ball was not to be interfered with when the city demolished it in December 1971 to use the site for an office building. Only thing I kept as a souvenir was the motor of the huge clock that was hanging inside on a wall. I use this as a sculpture, which reminds me and makes me proud that I played a little part in professional tennis history before the Open era of tennis, where even the first round player gets more than all the sixteen best players in the world at that time.

Virginia Slims in New York with Billie Jean King and Martina Navratilova, 1970

Virginia Slims

Casals, King, and Navratilova at Tennisport.

In 1970, the year before demolition of the Armory, Gladys Heldman, who was the first major promoter of women's tennis and the publisher of *World Tennis Magazine*, persuaded me to promote the first Virginia Slims invitational tournament in New York. This was another one of the few times I engaged in a major promotion. The history of the creation of the Virginia Slims tourneys was interesting. That September, eight of the world's leading female players had courageously turned down an invitation to play in the Pacific Southwest Championships in Southern California, protesting the inequity in prize money. The men were to receive twelve times as much as the women.

The women, with the help of Heldman's magazine, instead formed a tournament of their own in Houston that was sponsored by Virginia Slims and offered prizes of seventy- five hundred dollars. In response, the United States Lawn Tennis Association (USLTA) declared the female players to be contract pros, thereby prohibiting them from playing on USLTA teams and from being included in national rankings.

Gladys said that if I could offer fifteen thousand dollars in prize money, she would help me find a sponsor, which didn't happen, and I had to finance it myself, leaving me stuck with the contract. Interest among female players who were serious about tennis careers was instantaneous.

I had sixteen entrants for the tournament: Billie Jean King, Rosemary Casals, Valerie Ziegenfuss, Mary-Ann Curtis, Peaches Bartkowicz, Karen Krantzcke, Kerry Melville, Ann Haydon Jones, Denise Carter, Esme Emanuel, Tory Fretz, Francoise Durr, Stephanie DeFina Johnson, Ceci Martinez, Betty Ann Grubb Hansen, Judy Dalton, Pat Walker, and Kristy Pigeon.

In the end, I was sorry that I held that tournament. The players were not organized, and there were a lot of unnecessary arguments between the women. I promised myself that I would never do another event like that in the future. In later years, tournament directors decided that they did not need small entrepreneurs like me anyway because they could attract sponsors with bigger prize money. Today, even qualifiers get more money than I had put up for the total prize money in my tournament.

Annegret, who is a natural at public relations, was the quiet star during all the tournaments. It was easy for me to join in the entertainment she arranged after she did all the work—finding accommodations for players and their spouses, making dinner arrangements, and getting theater tickets and flowers. She kept them all in a good mood. She has a gift for making people feel welcome and special. She is like that to this day in our private lives, and wherever we are—in Wyoming, the Bahamas, or New York—hardly a day goes by that old friends or children of friends do not drop in to say hello, join us for a coffee or meal, or just catch up. It is Annegret's warmth that has been a constant welcome for the people we have met throughout our lives together.

Dustin Hoffman, taking lessons.

Natasha Richardson and Liam Neison.

*Ivan Lendl and I grew up in Ostrava and
played on the same Tennis Courts*

Exchanging Tennis for Golf lesson with James Bond (Sean Connery).

Mary Tyler-Moore and her husband spending their honeymoon playing tennis with Annegret and me.

Mary Tyler-Moore and her husband playing tennis with Annegret and I.

Becker practicing at Tennisport

Michael Douglas

Ken Roswall

Mayor John Lindsay

Major Dinkins

Guilarmo Villas.

Elton JOHN & David FROST

Elton John and David Frost at Tennisport Charity Tournament.

"Doris, put me in the game this afternoon"

I began looking for a desk secretary to arrange games for the players when I opened my first indoor called Tennis Inc., just like the efficient Ruth Unver had been doing for so many years at the River Club, where I taught. One of the applicants was Doris Pena, a beautiful young nineteen-year-old from Peru. Her English was very poor and, after two weeks, I lost patience and wanted to let her go. But Annegret, my wife, asked me to give her a chance for at least a few months to learn English "You will see that she will be okay," she said.

So I did, and for the last thirty-eight years, Doris has been the backbone of all my tennis clubs. I have never met such a patient and sensitive person with such a great personality and the innate ability to make customers smile. Her mind is like a computer; she remembers everything about the players: their qualifications, the names of their secretaries, and whom they liked or disliked, so that she very seldom paired a player up with someone who they would rather not play with. She found partners for everyone. If the shadow of eminent domain was the cloud over one shoulder, Doris Pena was the sunshine over the other. She has had the spirit, strength, and good cheer of Annegret, and she has remained loyal to our tennis enterprises although she has been offered many different jobs from competitions. Looking back, I don't know what I would have done without her.

Along with a desk secretary to book games and manage other administrative matters, there was one other person running the courts, the gentleman I had promised the job to in exchange for his having told me about the location. I was pleased that he had previously run the Bronx Armory. I believed the two of them would manage just fine while I continued teaching at the River Club, a job that I did not want to risk losing until I was sure that armory would work out financially. I was so busy teaching—and trusting—that during the construction, I relied only on regular telephone updates. It was my mistake to be only in phone contact with him. It is hard to detect a drinking problem on the phone.

Doris called me one day from the Tennisport and said she didn't know how to handle this case of husband and wife memberships.

During the beginning of the Women's Liberation Movement, I had just opened the Tennisport Club in Long Island City. My membership brochure contained husband and wife membership which was less than a single membership. One day while I was at the desk, two ladies approached me and asked for a husband and wife membership. I was very much surprised and didn't want to offend anyone so I asked them to show me their IRS report they filed together then I would give them the husband and wife membership. Refusing to show me they took me to court for almost a year at a very high expense and lost the case. I guess it was a test case for Gloria Steinman who was at the same time the leader of the Women's Liberation movement. There was no sense in going further to appeal and since then I changed all the brochures to single memberships.

Indoor and outdoor facility proposed at West Park Racquet Club. Now two apartment high rises.

C.V. Starr - "I Will Not Support Your Failure"

Finding affordable, available land in Manhattan or the boroughs is always a challenge, but while I had the armory facility, I began looking for a more permanent location, place to build my second club. I found three small city blocks of property at Ninety-Seventh Street and Columbus Avenue that belonged to the Alcoa Corporation. I managed to secure a seven-year lease and, with the savings I had, asked architect Harry Green to prepare the plans and permits for my new West Park Racquet Club. Things moved quickly. Within three months, we started to build, but I still needed funds to complete it. When I mentioned to C. V. Starr, who I considered to be then my good friend, that I needed forty thousand dollars to finish building the club, he declined. I needed it within a week to be able to open on time and not miss out on the summer season.

I went to C.V. Starr' office downtown on Maiden Lane to see him, but he was out of the country. His chief officer and member of the board, Gordon Tweedy, picked up the phone and connected me with him in Beirut, which was in those days a more meaningful gesture than a cross-Atlantic call in today's world. Again, I was at the raw end of a blow.

"I will not support your failure," he said, "but if you want to, why don't you try to buy a block of brownstones on the Upper East Side and build a big sports center, and I will finance that."

With the deadline looming, I was crestfallen but certain about his response. At the time, brownstones were in the fifty- to eighty-thousand-dollar range.

"Mr. Starr, that is very nice, but I still would only be your employee," I said. "I would like to own my own business." We said our good-byes and hung up.

"I am sorry," Tweedy said, "but that's how he is: unpredictable."

Later, Starr would give me credit for my decision. In the end, the absence of Starr's help opened the door for the help of Herb Lieberman, who later became my tax accountant and who never forgot my invitation when playing at the River Club. He cosigned the note, the rest of what I needed was loaned to me by Verena and Rod Cushman, who became very close friends since I arrived to New York and believed that the club will be a success. I managed to open the West Park Racquet Club with eleven outdoor tennis courts on time. The new club on the upper west side was a great hit in New York City. When it opened, our member list features many who were, at that time, at the beginning of great careers and would later become famous—George Soros, Barbara Streisand, Robert Redford, Gary Talese, Frank Stella, Clark Hulings, Mayor John Lindsay, and many others who were rising stars.

I remember George Soros sitting with me on the club terrace, and he said he didn't have a job and was looking for one. A few weeks later after a game, he approached me with a smiling face and said, "Freddie, I got a job at a bank." Soros, the Hungarian-born financier, would go on to gain fame for reportedly earning the most money in a day in currency trading against the British pound. It is fascinating to think that I was among the first to learn that he had landed a job in a bank. Since then, he has always joined my new tennis clubs.

Mayor John Lindsay was playing with me almost every morning from seven to eight before he went into the office. As a reward, Annegret and I were very often invited to official functions and parties. When I had my fiftieth birthday party at the famous Blue Angel nightclub, we were surprised at how funny and entertaining he was.

The demand for tennis was growing and already exceeded supply. I started to wonder if I could build an indoor club over those outdoor courts on the roof of the West Park Racquet Club. The combination could fulfill New York's needs year-round. I drew up plans and hired architect Harry Green and one of the best real estate lawyers in New York, Abe Lindenbaum. We tried for two years to get permission to build, but after dozens of meetings and much personal expense, the community board, all of our requests and applications were denied and I started not to trust the politicians and their promises.

Mayor Lindsay said he could not help us because it was a

community decision. One learns to live with disappointments. The indoor-outdoor courts would have been only thirty-five-feet high, or four stories. Now, thirty years later, there are skyscrapers on the site.

The Pan Am Girl

Being single and athletic, I was invited to many dinners and parties. Maybe the population statistics at the time were in my favor, but the need for an extra male at the dinner table was never-ending. And as a bachelor since my divorce from Margie, my interest in a good, home-cooked meal was also endless. Before one such party, a friend who was an employment officer for Pan Am set me up with a blind date to take to the party at his apartment. He told me to pick my dates up at Thirty-Third Street and Second Avenue, where four beautiful Pan Am stewardesses shared a brownstone apartment on the fourth floor of a walk-up. I did as instructed and took my dates and her to the cocktail party at the First Avenue apartment of our mutual friend.

One of the roommates was Annegret. We exchanged a few pleasantries at the cocktail party, and I later asked her for a date. I had fallen in love with her the moment I began to drive the girls to the party. On our first date, I told her that I was going to marry her. She said, "No way. You are too old for me, and, by the way, I am engaged to a man in Germany!" So it looked like I had lost the first set and had to try to win the next.

Her refusal only intrigued me more because it was dished out with such spark. This was a woman whose spirit and smile shone through. I was determined. And she was equally determined to discourage me if not to outright ignore me. Every time I asked her out, I had to take the other three girls along for the date. It did have a positive side. When we went to a restaurant, all the guys looked at me with envy since I was with four beautiful young women. One evening, I took them to dinner and to a John Jay ski movie.

Dina Merrill, with whom I played tennis often, happened to be in the seat just in front of us. She turned around and saw me. "Hi, Freddie," she said and kissed me on the cheek smiling.

One of Annegret's roommates, Dana, whispered to another, "We should have ordered steak instead of a burger, since we are in the company of such famous actors." We continued dating when she was in New York and corresponding when she was flying. On one occasion, when we were walking on Third Avenue, we stopped at a music shop and I bought her a record by Nat King Cole titled, "Love is the Thing." I asked her to come upstairs to my studio apartment at Fifty-Seventh Street and First Avenue and listen to it. She would not. Later, she found out that I did not even have a record player.

About a year later, in 1966, we got married in Hotel Plaza, where I had good connection with the food and beverage manager Beda Havelka very good friend of mine from Czech Republic. From there, we flew around the world on our honeymoon. Since she was a stewardess for Pan Am, she could purchase tickets for two hundred dollars each. We had a wonderful time. When we came back, her mother came to visit us. Apparently, my unabashed devotion to Annegret had done little to dissuade her of the idea that I was too old for her daughter. I invited them both to a Chinese restaurant in Manhattan and told Annegret what to select on the menu. She started to argue that she did not like the dish I ordered, but the waiter overheard and instructed her, "You'd better listen to your father!"

My mother-in-law beamed with one of those "I told you so" smirks. All at once, I knew I should have kept my mouth shut.

Communists Throwing out the Window Young Masaryk

I had known Dr. Karel Steinbach since I first arrived in the States. He had been a physician since World War II. Because he was Jewish and had seen the problems coming in 1938, he fled

Czechoslovakia and immigrated to England. He was a personal physician to Jan Masaryk. I met him in New York in 1953 at a Czech refugee function at the Czech restaurant Vasata at Seventy-Fourth Street and Second Avenue. It was the place where all the old Czechs and new immigrants met for the best roasted duckling and dumplings. The owner, Jarda Vasata, had a famous restaurant on Wenceslaus Square in Prague, and during the Nazi occupation, he helped to supply food the two Czech heroes in hiding. They had parachuted and successfully assassinated Heydrich, who was responsible for many thousands of Czechs being killed. I have always respected Jarda Vasata and his family, and they became my very close friends. Jarda was twenty years older than me, and we had a lot of stories to tell each other.

There is a great book, which describes the full story and the intriguing background of the Czech spy during that era titled: The Killing of SS Obergruppenfuhrer Reinhard Heydrich by Callum MacDonald.

Dr. Steinbach was a great intellectual, and he did charitable work for Czech organizations. Late in his life, he wrote a book in which he described how the Communists had imprisoned Jan Masaryk and then threw him out a window, claiming that he had jumped. Dr. Steinbach was the last person to have seen Masaryk, just half an hour before he died. He described In his book, that it was impossible that Masaryk would kill himself. The book was called *Witness Almost 100 Years Old*. Dr. Steinbach died when he was ninety-six.

Shirley Temple Black, US ambassador in Prague, and myself (right corner) with Czech President Vaclav Havel (front) at Kennedy Centre in Washington.

Being guest of Czech President Vaclav Klaus on Prague Castle

Visits to Czechoslovakia

In 1966, shortly after our honeymoon, I was finally able to visit my mother in Czechoslovakia. Though there had been a vast gap in our communication as I settled into a new life and she strived to survive in the life I had left behind eighteen years earlier, the homecoming was filled with emotion—crying and laughing, hugging, seeing old friends, and basking in a mother's love for her son and the son's love for his mother.

A few years later but still during the Communist regime and Alexander Dubcek era, my mother finally got a permit to visit Annegret and me in New York and meet our first child, Daniela. She translated Czech Fairy Tales into German, which I later put into a leather bound book, and has been kept as a family treasure for future generations. After that, she came every other year until she was eighty-six and unable to travel any longer. My children still remember when, in her eightieth year, she was still able to play the violin for us in the evening before bedtime. It has given me great joy to know that she lived to see and watch all three of her grandchildren grow. When she wasn't able to travel anymore, I would visit her in Ostrava at least twice a year, and I tried to make her life a little more comfortable by having a very faithful nurse and friend, Mrs. Hilda Grundelova and her family, take care of her in their house in Mistek, for which I am thankful.

Memorable Flight: Two Days, Frankfurt – New York

Heinz Nixdorf

On one of the flights in 1966, returning from a visit to my mother, a German couple sat next to me. They did not speak a word of English between them, and the lady was shaking and scared. Every time there was the slightest turbulence, she grabbed her husband's hand, and mine, too. *This is probably her first flight,*

I thought. To distract her from her anxiety, I started a conversation with them in German to their surprise and from then on, we talked all the way to New York. When we approached New York's JFK Airport (then called Idelwilde), the fog was so thick that the control tower ordered the plane to abort the landing and continue in the air. The pilot cruised for what seemed like a couple of hours and was still unable to land. He had to fly to Washington, DC to refuel. We returned once again to foggy New York, and still we were unable to land. We were all hungry and there was no food on the plane, so I offered to share Hungarian salami I had in my bag—I always traveled with one—to my new friends.

After circling New York late into the evening, the plane was finally re-routed to Montreal, where we were to spend the night at a motel near the airport. I knew Montreal from a previous visit, and since the German couple seemed so lost, I invited them to dinner at a very nice restaurant in town. Over these two days, we exchanged our life stories.

The husband, Heinz, told me that he was fond of Czechs because, after the war, when he was fleeing from the Eastern Front through Czechoslovakia, escaping from capture as a prisoner of war of the Red Army, Czechs hid him. They discarded his uniform, gave him civilian clothes, and told him how to reach his hometown of Paderborn. His gratitude toward Czechs in general and toward me for the little comfort I offered on that trip blossomed into another lifelong friendship.

The next morning, the flight was scheduled to leave for New York at 10:00 a.m. When the plane finally departed an hour late, the news came that New York was still shrouded in fog. In spite of the conditions, the pilot tried to land. He misjudged the runway and had to jerk the plane up at the last moment to avoid a watery landing in Jamaica Bay. Our final destination on this circuitous flight became Baltimore, where we landed in the late afternoon rain. From there, all the passengers boarded a bus to make the last leg of the trip. We finally arrived at the Forty-Second Street bus terminal, where I was met by Annegret. I had called her when we were in Baltimore, and three months pregnant at the time, she came there to welcome me home.

The German couple on the plane had introduced themselves as Heinz and Renate Nixdorf. After talking for about two days on the trip, we had grown really fond of one another. Heinz was involved in computer-manufacturing business ventures. He mentioned that he had started a company in Germany that had grown to employ a hundred people. Heinz's company, Nixdorf Computers, started off being privately owned by his family. Later, when it had grown to over thirty-six thousand employees, Nixdorf took it public, and since we were very good friends, he encouraged me to buy some shares in his new corporation. The stock doubled within two years, and I sold my shares when the value declined slightly. As a result, I was able to pay my obligations for the Tennisport operation. But that would come much later. And just as C. V. Starr had been my lifelong friend, Heinz Nixdorf became a part of our lives, enriching our way of life immeasurably. He was a brilliant man whose heart was golden.

The Nixdorf Institute, now the University of Paderborn in Germany, is a center for new thinking in the world of technology and home to several world-renowned learned professors and more than two hundred researchers. It carries Heinz's motto representing his social conscience: "Before we get to heaven, there's life on earth, and it is here that we must build a socially just society."

By the time I introduced the Nixdorfs to Annegret, who was also German origin, as we disembarked that unforgettable and fateful flight, we had all clicked. Heinz said he and Renate were on a business trip to Texas to purchase some new computer discs and asked if they could visit us on their way back. Unfortunately, we had to decline since we were planning to fly to Nassau in the Bahamas just three days later, the same time they were planning to return from Texas. Right away, Heinz asked, "Freddie, can we join you?" I responded happily, "Why not?"

The four of us spent a glorious week at the Balmoral in Nassau, Bahamas, where I gave Heinz and Renate their first tennis lessons. My Czech friend Ivor Petrak was the general manager at the

Balmoral Hotel, and he gave us a discount on the rooms. When it was time for us to leave, Heinz said that he would love to stay on for another week but admitted that he did not have enough money with him. He asked me to loan him twelve hundred dollars for the extended stay, which was all I had. On good faith, I lent him the cash. For this trip, I had taken all of our savings out of the bank because, at that time, credit cards were not much known. I always believed in living well, so my bank account was most of the time in my pocket. Annegret was horrified! How could I lend so much money to people we had known for only six days, she wanted to know. I told her, that I had learned in my life to recognize good characters in people and that I trusted them. So we went back to New York, and they stayed on in the Caribbean an additional week before returning to Germany. Almost nine months had passed, and we hadn't heard from them. Just as Annegret was bugging me about trusting people, an apology letter from Heinz arrived with a check for twelve hundred dollars. I never regretted it. It was the best investment of my life.

His tardiness with the check was certainly no indication of Heinz's business genius. There have been several books written about him and his company, and he became a well-known figure in German industry. Years after we met, when I was in need of additional funds to finance Tennisport, Heinz helped me with a loan to finish the clubhouse and the courts. After the first year of operations, Heinz stopped by to see the club. He was very impressed, but he had a question.

"Why don't you buy the land?" he said. "You are silly to pay rent."

"Heinz, it is the question that is silly," I replied. "I do not have the money or enough credit to buy the land."

He had the foresight and saw the opportunity to invest in real estate in the United States, especially with that view of Manhattan across the river. He said that he would finance it, and we could go fifty-fifty on the land. We bought seven acres, and over the years I paid him back with interest everything I owed him. His family remained a 50-percent partner on the land. We didn't have idea that thirty years later we will have to fight for fair market value following the government's taking it from us under what they called the rights of eminent domain. But let us not get ahead of ourselves in the story of tennis and immigrants in the land of opportunity.

Twenty Cows for My Wife

Leopard presented to my wife on the plantation in Tanzania by son of the owner, Liborious.

Over the years, the Boturs and Nixdorfs visited often and traveled together to many countries. Heinz also became the godfather to my son, Freddie Jr., in 1972, solidifying our family friendship. On one of our trips with them to Africa, we visited Kenya and then Tanzania. We flew from Nairobi by four-seater plane to Arusha. There the Nixdorfs had friends, the Gherkins, who had a large coffee plantation located seven thousand feet above sea level in the mountains. It was approximately three hours by jeep from Arusha, a very small town at the time of our visit. At the plantation that had previously been owned by a member of British royalty, also had a cement-based tennis court. On the second day of our visit Mr. Gherkins said that he had to visit the tribal chief as it is the duty of the owner to come and visit newly born babies. One of the tribal chief's wives had just given birth to a boy. We arrived to his hut, and he proudly showed us the boy. But the moment the chief saw Annegret, with her beautiful blond hair, he offered to buy her with all twenty of his cows. For the chief, it was a magnificent offer. Mr. Gherkin warned that it was not acceptable to offend the chief, so on Mr. Gherkins' advice, I countered with a request of fifty cows, knowing that he could not afford them. In this way, he saved face, and I "saved" my wife. It was a large and fascinating coffee plantation with also a few thousand feet lower where in because big plains and wildlife our host Mr. Gherkins wanted to show off how good of a shot he was and he took us to hunt for zebras (they hunted only to supply the meat for the employees). When we arrived to the area, Mr. Gherkins shot was not on the target and an animal was injured so we had to follow the trail tracking by jeep. At one point, we drove in the jeep, the father had told the son, don't drive straight, go more to the left because on the plain ahead of us was reflection from the heat like a mirage. He did not listen and two minutes later our jeep stopped in the sand and the jeep started to sink in the quicksand. So the truck which was following us with his staff had to pull us out. They found the dead zebra, his helpers said Muslim prayer before they parceled it and loaded it on the truck. When we came back from the hunt Mr. Gherkins wife, they all had scared faces because while we were away there were a few lions circling nearby and we left Heinz guarding them only with shotgun. It was a wonderful experience to see the coffee plantation and the difficult environment they lived in. Not only I almost lost my wife to the chief, but Gherkins had an eighteen-year-old son, Liborius, who fell in love with Annegret. He probably hadn't seen a white woman in ten years. And on the morning of our departure, he shot a leopard and sent the skin to the United States as a gift to her.

For the first time since I left Australia, I had a chance to visit it again. Heinz wanted the Australian government to get contract to mine coal, which would offset the challenge to meet demand that had risen because of the energy shortage that started in Europe in the 1980s. Negotiations failed because transporting coal from the middle of Australia to the harbors was almost impossibly expensive. Thirty years later, the Australian government did contract for coal mining, aided by new technology, transportation, and financing to bring it to ports with Chinese help.

Heinz always referred to me as part of his family. His three young sons spent many summer vacations at our home on Long Island learning English, traveling, and gaining an understanding about life in the States. While Heinz and Renate, for all their achievements, learned only some English, they understood the importance of their children learning more.

God's Country: Wyoming

One day, Annegret suggested that the Boturs and the Nixdorfs travel out west. Annegret's uncle had taken her on a trip to Wyoming in 1962 when she studied in Greenville, South Carolina, and the open beauty of the land moved her. She has written an interesting article about the West and cowboys for a German newspaper that time (I had the article framed, and it is hanging in our house in Jackson Hole.) So I arranged a trip to Jackson Hole, Wyoming, and we hired a guide and cowboys to take us camping in the wilderness. It had a tremendous impact on Heinz, who immediately loved Wyoming and began referring to it as "God's country," even though we spent six or seven hours a day in the saddle and having the opportunity to see all the wildlife. I remember watching my son, Freddie, as a six-year-old, falling asleep as he was riding and not falling off. The Nixdorfs' kids loved it, too, especially when I bought Heinz's son Mathias a 9mm Colt from one of the cowboys as memento from the "wild" West.

Our family in past years accompanied the Nixdorfs to the Grand Canyon, Kenya, and Tanzania. Once, I even joined his team on a business trip to Brazil, where Heinz bought a large mahogany forest as part of a plan to build a village and export rare wood to Europe. After investing quite a large sum, he encountered what he termed "Brazilian intrigue" and sold the forest back to the government ten years later for one dollar.

On different occasions before introducing them to Wyoming and when all of our children had school vacations, we traveled to Banff Springs Hotel in the Canadian Rockies, where my very close friend, Ivor Petrak, was now the general manager and VP of Canadian Pacific Hotels. He was very helpful in arranging our cowboy packing trips on horses in the wilderness.

Bavarian Prime Minister Strauss in New York Court.

Ivor was one of several Czech friends in the hospitality industry, who enjoyed success in hotels or country clubs, and I always wondered if it had to do with how we were brought up to welcome others into our homes. My close friend Emil Ransdorf after his dramatic escape from Czech Republic, who now after being with me in the DP camp at Schwabach and at 111 Furtherstrasse in Nuremberg became the manager of the Howard Johnson Red Coach Grill on Broadway. Howard Johnson personally praised Emil as one of the best managers in his company; he told me this one day after playing at Tennisport. Another friend, B. Havelka, became the food and beverage manager at the Plaza in New York and arranged our wedding party there. L. Vomacka was the manager of the Woodmere Golf Club, and another Waldorf Astorias chef Lejcek retired from the hotel and opened a motel and restaurant in Lake Placid called Chatteau Prague. Many other Czechs and Slovakian emigrants wound up in the hospitality industry. One of my closest friends the most successful Slovakian emigrant hotelier, is Henry Kallen in New York. We all kept in touch for many years.

We shared so many adventures and experiences with our dear friends, the Nixdorfs, during our forty years of friendship. Heinz's passing in 1986 left a gap in our lives that we still feel after all these years, though we are still in touch with members of his family.

His primary business was left in the good hands of Klaus Luft, who had worked with Nixdorf Computer AG since 1979 in several positions, including finance and marketing. He was on the board, a post he held until the company was sold to Siemens in 1999. Luft was well recognized in the world of technology and has gone on to serve as a director at Dell and on the advisory board of Goldman Sachs. He was instrumental, through my city connections, in finding the location for the Nixdorf Corporation on Third Avenue and 54th Street in New York. In another instance, I made arrangements at the criminal court with Mayor Lindsey for Bavarian Foreign Minister Franz Josef Strauss who was robbed and insisted to prosecute the case next day. In Mayor Lindsay's administration I assisted in locating office space, and it was the City of New York's tax coffers that benefitted as a result. Few years later when there was a German delegation visiting Washington, DC, Heinz Nixdorf was honored by President Reagan.

Parker Ranch (Botur Inc.), Colorado

From the first time we visited Wyoming together, Heinz talked about buying property there, although he had already bought a large ranch in the Parker suburb of Denver, Colorado, for a housing development in which I, as an American, had to participate in to determine ownership to meet the legal requirements. The corporation had to be called Botur Inc., though I had only a one-percent share and the property was called Parker Ranch, and Heinz started big development with several hundred reasonably prized houses.

Unfortunately, my dear friend died of a heart attack before he could fulfill the Colorado development dream. Our family lost a best friend. We still keep in touch almost on a weekly basis with Mrs. Nixdorf, who, now a widow, enjoys all eight of her grandchildren. Their sons Martin and Mathias, have a second home in Florida where there are in touch regularly with my daughter, Andrea, who lives nearby.

With Heinz's death, I told myself that I was not going to wait any more. With my son Freddie I went to Jackson Hole to look at properties, but didn't make any decisions. On the way back to the airport, the agent said, "There is a beautiful corner in Jackson Hole—about twelve acres with a view of the Tetons. It has been for sale for two years and has a nice house on it. Why don't you look?" Long story short, I negotiated a good price, and since then Wyoming has become our new home and residence for our family. I was very excited after signing the deal, so I decided to spend my first night in my new home, bought a sleeping bag, and happily fell asleep in it. About an hour later, I woke to something tickling me. I jumped up and saw a dozen mice having a good time, so I went to the hotel. The next day, I bought a few dozen mousetraps and two cats to clear the two-year-empty house of them.

Investment with Czech Refugees

My friend Capek came to me one day with exciting news that he has met Czech inventor by name J. Ruzicka. He escaped from the Czech Republic with his invention of how to make mica paper. Before his invention mica which has been used for many years as an insulating mineral rock product which was not flexible. The inventor had a patent on how to make paper out of it for practical use. It sounded very exciting. Capek's company was called I.D.E. (International Development Engineers) in Queens. We formed a partnership for the Mica paper which Capek, close friend of mine Jim Donovan (friend from River Club) and Herb Lieberman (my tax accountant) and I tried to market it. Capek has flown to Switzerland and confirmed with Brown Bovery engineering company that machinery for the Mica paper can be made and they were willing to make a pilot plant. First we had a client in Ireland, then in Taiwan where Herb Lieberman and I made two unsuccessful trips meeting top Taiwanese government officials. After that, we offered it to Heinz Nixdorf who contacted Siemens Corporation in Germany and they were interested.

During this period, we opened our office on 400 Park Avenue on 17th floor. Thanks to Jim Donovan. Later I found it used to be Jackie Kennedy's office before. Our lease was only month to month basis. Nixdorf made already arrangements with the chairman of Siemen's A.G. to meet me with the proposal at the airport in Frankfurt. Unfortunately the night before I was supposed to meet Nixdorf and the chairman of Sieman's Corporation at the airport in Frankfurt, we had a meeting with the inventor Mr. Ruzicka. He started to make for the second time unreasonable large demands in the contract. I had to make a decision. If the inventor started the demands with us, it would be very difficult, knowing Heinz Nixdorf and his strict business discipline to get along in the future with the inventor Ruzicka.

So I decided rather lose the project, than to lose my friend Heinz. I picked up the phone and even though it was 2am in Germany I called and cancelled the meeting, at the same time ended our relationship with the inventor and dissolved our corporation. Later Heinz respected my decision even it was embarrassing for him to cancel the appointment. It was another learning experience. I don't think would be possible to do enterprise like that freely in any socialistic country as it was in the United States for Capek and me the two Czech refugees. Of course learning is a difficult process and I didn't give up even after Mica failure as I found out on the next case which was.....

In the 1970s, the boom days of tennis were just dawning, and I was happy to serve as a link to other Czechs. I had given and received help from countrymen, and I had made lifelong friends. So when I was introduced to a Czech inventor, Professor Krcma, who was visiting the United States in search of financing for his process of recycling old carpets to make new materials, I listened intently and then plowed right in, tempted as always to trust a fellow Czech. Plus, the man was clearly well educated, had a likeable face, and was referred to me by one of my Czech employees, Frank Mellon, a former employee of Radio Free Europe in Munich. Mellon was confident enough that he personally invested a sizable sum in the professor's plan. I invested too. Professor Krcma's invention later proved not to be what he said it was. We think that he tried to sell the same scheme to other people. Regardless, he vanished, never to be heard from again, even though we had all the contracts to his patents.

Vlastimil Koubek (Washington DC Architect) – A 1992 Reunion

There were so many bright moments in the early nineties, including a completely unexpected reunion with a childhood friend. When I was going to high school in Ostrava in 1940, Vlastimil Koubek and I dated the same girl at the same time, though neither of us knew it until later when she dropped us. Koubek and I became good friends. Like all young people did then, we had good, easygoing times— going to coffee houses and wine cellars, dating, and dancing. At that time, there were no laws against young people's drinking beer. I lost touch with Vlastimil until 1992.

That year, Annegret surprised me with a seventieth birthday party at the famed Rainbow Room on the sixty-fifth floor of the GE Building in Rockefeller Center, a world-renowned location that, sadly, closed in the height of the recession in 2009. But the night of the party was unforgettable.

Annegret had invited more than one hundred people, all of whom were eating, drinking, and dancing to the music of the Peter Duchin orchestra, and there, among the crowd, was my childhood friend from Czechoslovakia. We hugged, and I don't know whether I laughed or cried harder. That is when I discovered that Vlastimil had become one of the most successful commercial architects in Washington, DC, having designed ninety-nine office buildings in the city and become very well connected politically and socially.

Upon his death in 2003, the *Washington Post* wrote:

"Vlastimil Koubek, 75, one of Washington's most influential architects whose work on nearly 100 offices, hotels and apartment buildings since the late 1950s helped to shape the city's skyline, died of cancer on February 15 at his home in Arlington. In one of his larger projects, he partnered with the world-famous architect IM Pei, and in another, Hyde Park, he was credited with bringing clean lines and modern design to a city that had been awash in cornices and crannies."

It gave me tremendous satisfaction and a sense of wonder to know that a friend from our little town Ostrava in Czechoslovakia had "helped to shape the city's skyline" in the capital of the great United States of America. In 1985, *Washingtonian* magazine named my old friend one of twenty notable Washingtonians "who in the past twenty years had the greatest impact on the way we live and who forever altered the look of Washington."

Chapter Five:
Learning about Auctions

I Owned a Moose

By my second year at the River Club, I usually found myself free between the hours of noon and two o'clock, so I walked through the nearby neighborhoods. Once, I was all the way to Fifty-Ninth Street between Third Avenue and Lexington, where I stopped in front of a large window. Through the glass I saw people sitting in rows of chairs and raising their hands in the air. A red flag with the word *Auction* was hanging outside the door. I had no idea what it meant. I had never encountered anything like it—not in Czechoslovakia, other parts of Europe, Australia, even America up to that time. Out of curiosity, I went in, found a seat, and watched. A man would hold out an item, and people would raise their hands and, in this way, buy the item. To someone who had never seen anything like this before, the auction was fascinating. It must have been premonition of moving to Wyoming wildlife. The concept of buying through bidding against strangers was foreign to me. But it held my attention in a way that was almost hypnotic. Then on the stage appeared the most beautiful stuffed moose head I had ever seen. The moose looked at me with his glass eyes, and I was hypnotized. The auctioneer called out, "Who gives me a hundred? Who gives me fifty?"

My hand shot up at thirty dollars (that time about three tennis lessons) and that was the first auction buy of my life. I owned a moose. As quickly as I had bought it, I realized I had no place to put it, so I never picked it up. But that was the beginning of my passion for auctions. Whenever the chance came to buy small items, whether they were Greek vases, Chinese marble tabletops, paintings, small tables, or other unusual items that spoke of a certain culture or exotic place, I'd take them. I stored my purchases in the garage of my first house in Cedarhurst, on the Long Island. Coming home one evening years later, I found Annegret beaming.

"Darling, now you can put your car in the garage!" she said proudly. "I called Sanitation and had it cleaned—all those broken things and that stuff you had!" What could I do? Just seeing that smiling, happy face, radiating with pleasure over the wonderful thing she thought she had done for me.

In any case, after that I found auctions that handled a higher quality of goods. I learned a lot from attending auctions—a little about art and objet d'art, but more important, perhaps, I learned how little all the things we collect in our lives mean when you sell your house and have to get rid of your 50 years of collected passionate items. From these auctions, though I and anyone else who ever haunts auctions has to be honest and admit that we have, from time to time, bought junk that we lugged home just for the sheer joy of outbidding someone else.

One auction in New York was held to disseminate the estate of a famous television announcer, David Susskind, who died in 1987. A news commentator for CBS, he was an avid and serious collector of Western art and a friend of a famous Western artist named C. M. Russell. I saw a piece by Albert Bierstadt, one of the top American West artists. I bid on it and went as high as sixty thousand dollars, not knowing for sure how I would raise the money. I breathed a sigh of relief that outweighed the tinge of disappointment when the bidding went higher.

But I wanted to buy something at this auction. I felt as though I knew David because I had watched him so often on TV, and owning something that he had once owned held an appeal. Over in a corner was a box of "junk" with horns sticking out. I looked in and saw African kudu horns and a buffalo skull. The box cost me about fifty dollars. I brought it home and left it in the cellar of the house. That was years before I had any idea that I would own a house in Wyoming. When we moved to Jackson Hole, I took the buffalo skull along because I thought it would be perfect to hang somewhere. Ten years later, I saw a few Bierstadt paintings at the National Museum of Wildlife Art in Jackson Hole, but I was pretty sure I was the only one in Jackson Hole who had African kudu horns and a buffalo skull that once belonged to TV journalist David Susskind.

During the construction of the Jackson Hole house, the builder came to me and said, "Mr. Botur, I will give you five hundred dollars for the buffalo skull."

I said, "You must be joking."

"What do you want, a thousand for it?" he replied. "You know what you have."

I went down to the cellar to look at the buffalo head. The skull was original. It was the inspiration for the symbol of Charles Marion Russell, a very famous western painter. The skull is included on most of his paintings and drawings. It had his original signature on the forehead. That skull is priceless and is now hanging in our living room in Jackson Hole.

My greatest experience at auctions was when Heinz Nixdorf called me and said, "Freddie, I would like you to attend a Sotheby's auction and bid for me on one painting by Max Beckmann. It's a portrait of a woman that I like very much."

So I went to the auction. It was very exciting, as it was the first time in my life to sit with art dealers who were bidding for paintings by artists like Matisse and Rembrandt and the first time that I, a Czech tennis pro who had never even heard of an auction until a few years before, was trusted to act as someone's agent. When the Beckman portrait of a lady came up for bid, I just held the card up until I bought it for a hundred and twenty thousand. I called up Heinz with the news, and he was very happy about it. The family kept the painting after Heinz passed away, and it hangs in one of his rooms in the home in Paderborn, the town where he was born in Germany.

While visiting my mother in Communist Czechoslovakia in the 1970s, during Alexander Dubcek's brief era, I dropped in on some friends who were artists. One of them was Bedrich Dlouhy. He had been recommended to me by my tennis pro Jitka Volavkova, he was a professor of art at Prague University and a very well-known painter. I visited his studio, where he showed me a beautiful painting of geese on a lake that was eight feet by twelve feet. He had completed only a small part of it, but I liked it. At that time, American dollars meant a lot in Communist countries, and I bought the unfinished painting for a very reasonable price.

It took Dlouhy another three years to finish it. I had him send it to New York, and in the eighties, it was on exhibit at my Tennisport gallery, where it was greatly admired. The New York *Times* even ran a picture of it and an article in its Art section. It had been hanging for five years when the curator of the National Gallery of Prague, a Mr. Krizak, visited me and asked if I would loan it to the Czech National Museum in Prague. He said the museum would pay for the transportation, so I loaned it to them for three years. The painting of the geese was so large that I really didn't have a good place to hang it. And after Tennisport closed, it was too large to hang in our house. I finally sold it to a gallery in Prague, where it was bought by a collector of Dlouhy's paintings. It hangs now where it belongs—in a Czech castle.

In the meantime, I acquired a few more of Dlouhy's works, including a portrait of the painter's wife, which once hung in the office of Czech president Vaclav Havel. The same buyer who bought the painting of the geese bought this one as well. I still have two of Dlouhy's paintings—one of a forest scene and a smaller one of his painting tools. They are in my home, and I will never sell them. To this day, Dlouhy is considered one of the great artists of the Czech Republic, and I am honored and humbled that circumstances in my life led to my owning and caring for these two paintings.

After the Communists were defeated in the Velvet Revolution of 1989, I asked Professor Dlouhy to recommend one of his thirty students to paint a piece of Western art for our home in Wyoming. He recommended several, and I chose a man named Honza Pistek to come to out to our ranch. Over a period of about two months, he painted a dozen beautiful scenes at the ranch—cowboys, Native

Americans, and animals. A few years later, Pistek had become a very successful painter in Prague and was also involved in the production of films.

Tennis Courts Closed for the Art Show

Closing of West Part Racket club for exhibition of stranded artists.

My connection to art deepened with passing years. In the late sixties, I was watching television and happened to catch a news story about a group of artists who had come all the way from Italy to New York to stage an exhibit of their work in Central Park. Just before they were due to set up, they discovered that the company that sold them the package trip to the United States had never gotten them a city permit to exhibit their art. I felt so sorry for them that I immediately called the TV station and got in touch with the group. I closed the West Park Racquet Club to tennis that Sunday, invited my members, spread the word, and hosted the exhibition there. They sold enough paintings, including two that I bought, to pay their way back to Italy, and they left the United States happy for having made the trip. I still have pictures of the event.

This was not my only brush with art at West Park. A very

enthusiastic tennis player rented an apartment about 150 feet from the main tennis court so he could be close to our clubhouse. When we called him to play, he would just lean out his window and yell, "I'm coming down!"

His name was Frank Stella. At the time, I had no idea that he was also a famous artist. He and his friend, architect Richard Meier, battled on my tennis courts at the West Park Racquet Club and, for many years before its closing, at Tennisport.

A Struggling Artist

I do not know whether it was coincidence or fate, but art and artists seemed to be running a close second to tennis in my life, and in the 1972, after I had opened Tennisport in Long Island City, I was approached by a young Serbian boy searching for a job. He said he was an artist but needed work and would be willing to do just about anything to earn money honestly. I gave him a job brushing the courts and giving general assistance. He was diligent, hardworking, and serious about his art. After hours on the court, even in the heat of summer, he would

An original Dukovic painting from the time while he worked for Tennisport in New York in the early 70s.

change, dress, and go to town to visit galleries and museums. One day he asked me if he could use one of the garages in the back of the club so that he could paint. I happily gave him use of the space. He was with us for two or three years and left me about seven of the paintings that he had done during that time. One day he came to me and said he was leaving for San Francisco. I wished him good luck and didn't hear from him for thirty years after the day he left.

None of us could remember his name or where he was—even Doris couldn't recall—but from time to time I wondered what became of him. In November 2010, I received an e-mail from a fellow by the name Dukovic. He said how sorry he was to hear that our Tennisport, where he had worked for a couple of years and the place that had given him a start in America, was closed because of eminent domain. This was the boy I had been wondering about, hoping for his success and happiness. He is now fifty-six and still living in San Francisco. He is also still an artist looking for recognition, waiting to be discovered. I wish him good luck.

Fascinating Artist Chiang Er-Shih

Chiang Er-Shi.

One of the most interesting people who joined the West Park Racquet Club was the Chinese artist Chiang Er-Shih. He and his wife would end up playing a role in my life that was unlike any I would have ever imagined, both for the friendship and experience and for what became the ultimate financial problem. That Er-Shih was a respected artist was undisputed. Hugo Munsterberg, an art history professor, said Chiang Er-Shih "recaptured the spirit of the great ancient heritage." In a catalog of Er-Shih's paintings, Munsterberg describes them as being "executed with a beautiful feeling." An art expert in Tokyo told me that "Mr. Chiang follows in the footsteps of the best Chinese painters. He is a master of landscape, which is to the Chinese the highest form of painting." The expert compared Er-Shih's work to the early study of the four Wang dynasties. Other experts spoke readily of his ability to capture the indefinable beauty of the Chinese landscape, and the Tokyo National Museum once referred to him as "foremost among contemporary Chinese painters."

Everything I learned about Er-Shih reinforced his standing in the lofty world of fine art. It was probably all true and set a perfect interest for me, having heard talk of art deals but knowing little of what was behind those deals. I was a primed victim, innocent and impressed, ready to walk headlong into the trap that opened wider as the friendship between our families grew stronger.

We met Er-Shih when he joined the West Park Racquet Club. His wife, Rosemary, was a tall, beautiful, European-born-and-bred blonde who, like many Swiss, spoke perfect German. With Annegret's first language being German, the two wives—both of whom were considerably younger than their husbands—became fast friends and played tennis frequently. I admired Er-Shih, who was intelligent, always elegantly dressed, and graced with impeccable manners and charm. Very tall for someone of Chinese descent, he seemed to have an air of gentility about him, and it was rumored that he had lived a very interesting early life, though no one seemed to know the details of his past. In one story, he had been a pilot for Chiang Kai-shek. In another, his father had been an ambassador in Berlin during the Hitler regime. Either or both could have been true. It seemed probable that his family had been well known and well-to-do in Chinese society prior to Chiang Kai-shek's death in 1975. In the United States, the artist and his stunning wife lived well in a lovely New York apartment, moved in social circles, and continued to be well connected in the world of fine art and cuisine, including an impressive close friendship with Peggy Guggenheim.

In fact, he often dined in New York with Ms. Guggenheim and her friend, Mrs. Vander Mael, accompanied by Tom Connors from St. Croix. He lived in the Caribbean Islands and had been an officer in the US Army with General McArthur in Tokyo after the war. Along with seeing Er-Shih and his wife at the tennis club, he often invited us to dinners in Chinatown in New York City. He usually called the chef two days ahead to arrange for the preparation of a traditional Chinese feast for twelve to fourteen people. Never have I eaten better Chinese dishes than those at his parties.

Several times, Er-Shih mentioned that he had a valuable family collection of Chinese art scrolls dating from the thirteenth to the fifteenth centuries. I didn't pay much attention at first. He also said that he had started out at sixteen as a classical Chinese artist, studying masterpieces and attempting to re-create them. Later, he moved to the region of Chiang-nan on the banks of Yangtze River, famous for its scenic beauty. It was the majesty of that landscape, he said, that inspired his work.

Er-Shih enjoyed tennis, and we enjoyed each other's company, especially when he mentioned Mortimer Sackler and his daughter Kathe, who were members of my club and were also great collectors of Asian Art. Annegret and I were invited by Mortimer to play tennis and attend parties with them in southern France one summer, events which one doesn't forget and treasure the memories. Amazing almost scary is that Er-Shih gave me small watercolor painting a few years before he died on the countryside where he was actually buried. While I am typing the story the painting hangs on the wall next to me.

Er-Shih had a condominium in Lucerne, Switzerland, and a house in Marbella, Spain. Since he was about five years older than me, at the end of a tennis match, we sat down and talked. I liked to listen to him, and we exchanged stories of our grandfathers and our pasts. During the second year of our friendship, I told him that Annegret and I were going to Europe with our daughters, and he insisted that we go to Switzerland and stay with him. We accepted and had a great time playing tennis at a beautiful tennis club not far from his condo in Lucerne. From there, Annegret and I wanted to take our daughters to Italy. Again, Er-Shih was the perfect gentleman and host, insisting that we take his convertible, a Mercedes 280SL. Unfortunately, we left Lucerne later than we should have, and as we drove over the Alps into Italy, it was dark. The girls, who were four and five then, began getting restless, so I searched for a place to stay overnight. I had not made any reservations, and the hotels along the road were booked. But at one, the desk clerk told me that if we drove five kilometers through this forest, we'd find a farm that usually took people overnight.

When we arrived, we discovered a tiny cottage next to the barn. The place smelled from the cows' bodily functions, but who were we to be fussy when it was late? The girls were tired, the farmer and his wife were very charming, and they were happy to have guests. To my surprise, when I went to the outhouse, about ten meters away from the house, I found not toilet paper but pieces of newspapers dated 1933, so I had a little time to catch up on history.

Our beds were covered with goose-down quilts about ten inches thick and soaked by both humidity and the smell of the farm. The next morning, our daughters got to watch the farmer milking the cows for our breakfast. The girls hardly touched it as it was different from pasteurized milk and had the cows' hair and smell of where it had just come from. I think I paid about five dollars for all of us, including the breakfast.

As we were trying to get back to the highway, not far from the farm and way back in the mountains, surrounded by majestic scenery, we passed a beautiful wooden church. It was a Sunday morning, and there must have been at least a hundred people pouring out as we stopped to watch the procession. My children had learned the German fairy tales about Heidi in the mountains, and suddenly, there in full folk costume, was a very pretty twelve-year-old girl with long braided blond hair leaving the church. Annegret said to the children, "You see, there is Heidi!" The girls believed it. It certainly captured the spirit of the story to see her there.

We continued driving through the Bremer Pass and back to Lucerne. When I returned the car to Rosemary, she exclaimed, "What did they do to my dashboard?"

The children had bitten into the fresh, beautiful leather.

Annegret and I were embarrassed.

When we got back to New York, I thanked Er-Shih for treating us to such a wonderful time. Over time, we had more good dinners and continued to be close friends. Since I traveled to Hong Kong quite a bit with C. V. Starr and had met many Chinese intellectuals and businessmen, I thought I was beginning to know the Chinese character and personality. Among the people I met, Er-Shih stood out. He was, by any measure, an incredible person of immense talent and intelligence. He told great stories, some of which were about ghosts, not surprising since Chinese people believe in ghosts and are very superstitious.

At about the same time, 1970, Er-Shih was having an exhibition at the Art Institute in Chicago. He invited me, and I gladly accepted. It was fascinating to meet people from different walks of life who had come to see my friend's work, an experience that increased my faith in him and his Chinese paintings. He shared catalogs of his earlier exhibitions with me, including one from his 1954 exhibition in Tokyo. I still have those catalogs. Why would I question the value of his own collection of older works?

Over the years, Er-Shih had occasionally offered to sell me a scroll. I bought a few and have some of them in my house. Some of the scrolls were for my personal collection, which was just beginning to grow under his tutelage. Others, he suggested, we could sell at auction at Christie's for between forty and fifty thousand dollars. They did. So I made a few dollars through the auctions at which I was no longer raising my hand but waiting for others to raise theirs. Again, compared to making fifteen dollars an hour teaching tennis, it seemed amazing, and I was grateful to my friend for letting me share in the good fortune. I financed my initial purchase, which seemed a small price to pay for the return on investment. Er-Shih claimed that one of the scrolls was very valuable but said he would let me have it for a third of its price, so I kept it.

He led me gently into the fold, though I hardly recognized it at the time because it was handled with his usual charm. "You are such a wonderful friend to me," he said one day. "I am going to let you in on a couple of my art deals."

Avery Brundage's (Collector of Chinese Art and President of Olympic Committee) Note Payable One Year Later

At times Er-Shih would arrive at the club with beautiful jade vases or figures. Some of the vases were paper thin and among the most beautiful things I had ever seen. He told me that he was a friend of Avery Brundage, the Chicago industrialist who had been chairman of the International Olympic Committee for thirty years and had amassed one of the greatest collections of Asian art in the world. Today, that collection is the basis of the Asian Art Museum of San Francisco, with priceless art and artifacts spanning six thousand years. Er-Shih said he traveled to San Francisco to sell to Brundage.

Er-Shih told me about how Brundage handled his purchases, paying with a "note payable" one year after the date of purchase. I trusted Er-Shih when he presented me with a note from Brundage for a hundred thousand dollars and asked me to get my bank, Chase Manhattan, to discount it and pay him cash ahead of time. Again, why wouldn't I? Discounting notes for early payment was not unusual. My banker at the Park Avenue branch of Chase Manhattan, Harmon Butler, whom Er-Shih had occasionally invited to dinners with us, asked me to cosign the note when I took it to him.

About nine months later, Er-Shih came in with another note for $150,000. Again, this didn't seem like a problem. I was reassured when Harmon told me that Er-Shih had redeemed all of his previous notes ahead of time.

Partnership in Collection at the Musee Cernuschi in Paris

Around this time, Er-Shih told me he was going to stage an exhibition of his family's art collection in Paris at the Musee Cernuschi, well known for Asian art. He had taken the family's collection to be certified and appraised by Frank Caro Gallery on Fifty-Seventh Street in New York. He showed me the list of his thirty-two Chinese scrolls, which were appraised by Frank Caro at over $1 million. Er-Shih said a Chinese art collector from Chicago named Mrs. Regenstein would offer $2.5 million for the art collection after the exhibition in Paris. I learned that Joseph and Helen Regenstein had a priceless collection of art and music, again reaffirming Er-Shih's connections. My friend offered me the chance to buy 30 percent of the collection. I asked why he was making me such a generous offer.

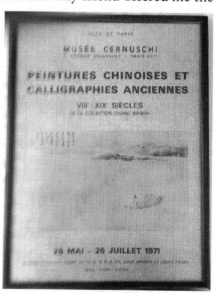

"I want you to make some money. It's an easier way than running after the tennis ball," he said, "and you are a good friend."

I arranged a few loans, which I was able to get given the now- booming business of tennis and my own net worth, and paid him $350,000. He signed on the side of the appraisal that I owned 30 percent of the collection.

Brochure of my involvement in Er-Shih Collection in Paris.

I flew to Paris for the opening of the exhibition at the Museum Cernuschi of what was now "our" collection. The exhibition would be in place for about six weeks. I still have the catalogs from the exhibition as a reminder of our days of glory in Paris, where we were received with great honor and invited to a few dinner parties.

I cannot lie—I enjoyed the limelight tremendously, as well as the privilege of walking through the museum and admiring our exhibit.

During the exhibition, Er-Shih came to me and said he had just sold Avery Brundage some porcelain for a $350,000 note, payable eleven months from then. I trusted him. There had been no problems with our previous dealings, and I had seen Avery Brundage's signatures on previous notes and had seen his notes confirmed by Brundage's bank in Chicago, so I told Harmon Butler to go ahead and discount it. I cosigned the note.

Everything seemed to be in order until about five days after the note was signed and the $350,000 had been discounted. Butler called me and said, "Freddie, I just got a phone call from Avery Brundage's bank in Chicago. A secretary claims that Mr. Brundage hasn't bought anything from Chiang Er-Shih in the last few years."

"I cannot believe it," I said. "This is almost impossible."

I called Er-Shih right away at his home in Marbella, Spain, where he played tennis at my friends Lew Hoad's club in Toremolinos. Er-Shih answered, "There must be some mistake. This is impossible! Freddie, you should not worry since somebody must be lying."

I told him I could not afford to pay for the $350,000 note if it defaulted, it would be disastrous. I had only a little cash in the bank, and now a $350,000 note was hanging over me. I was panicky.

"This could finish me, Er-Shih," I told him. "Something is horribly wrong."

"Don't worry about it," Er-Shih said calmly and coolly. "I'll call up the bank."

Despite his words of reassurance, I wasn't buying it. I could not understand why Brundage would claim that he had not signed any notes and had not done business with Er-Shih for the last few years if he had. For a few seemingly endless and sleepless nights, I tossed and turned fitfully, trying to figure out what had gone wrong and how. To my surprise, on the fourth day, Harmon Butler called me and said that the note had been paid. To say that I was overcome with relief is an understatement. I heaved audible sighs of relief. We (or I, to be more specific), with my dreams of dabbling in the world of rare art, had come within inches of losing everything I had worked for.

Er-Shih on a Marble Table

About a week later, I got a phone call from Rosemary. Er-Shih had just died on the tennis court at Lew Hoad's tennis club from a massive heart attack.

He could have wiped us out, but strangely I still considered myself his very good friend. He had paid the loan back, and we still owned our collection. I was devastated at the news of his death, and I felt sorry for his widow. The next day, I caught a flight to Marbella and met with Rosemary, Peggy Guggenheim, her friend Tom, and Lilly (Er-Shih's daughter from his first marriage, which I knew nothing about before his death). Rosemary was heartbroken, crying uncontrollably, hugging me, and thanking me for being such a close friend. I stayed overnight in a hotel, and the next day I was asked to identify Er-Shih's body. I didn't know why.

Spanish officials took me into the hilly part of Marbella, where there was a cemetery and a morgue. Walking into the morgue was like playing a scene in a movie with Frankenstein's monster. There, on a marble table in the narrow, dark room with one small window, was Er-Shih's naked body. He had been dead only two days and already he looked like a wax figure. I looked at my friend and two thoughts crossed my mind: One carried me back more than half a century to the time I had to look at my grandmother's and uncle's dead bodies. I swallowed hard and pushed the memory away. The other was harder to ignore. Er-Shih reminded me of one of the ghosts he spoke about, matter-of-factly stating that he had seen them as if to him ghosts were a part of life. I signed the paper and walked out. Now I knew why no one in the family wanted to or was able to face the corpse of one of their own, why it was left for me to close the door on the last sight of this man who had strode through our lives. The funeral was held the next day. Er-Shih was in a closed casket. Outside the morgue, two men pushed a four-wheeled carriage through the cemetery. There were only six of us accompanying the casket. A priest said a few words, and besides him, I was the only one who said good-bye to Er-Shih with a brief eulogy.

I thought Er-Shih would be buried somewhere in the cemetery, but to my surprise we followed the casket all the way to the end of the cemetery, where there was a gate. We went through the gate and, about fifty feet further on, came to a big wall with openings just big enough to put caskets in. There were hundreds of compartments. The pallbearers put the casket into one of those compartments. There wasn't even a name on the casket, or perhaps in all the movement I didn't notice. That was the end of it. What a shock. I did not know then that, in Spain, if you are not Catholic, you cannot be buried in the official cemeteries.

After analyzing the case with a few people, I reasoned that Er-Shih may have taken pills before going to play tennis and thus had intentionally taken his own life. He was in debt and wanted to save face because he would have had to go into hiding, as is the Chinese custom. In the 1970s in Spain, people were not trained to investigate how heart attacks occurred. No autopsy was requested, and none was performed. Over the years, I have tried to sort out the business of Er-Shih—the combination of intelligence and talent and a lifestyle that overwhelmed the ability to pay for it. I do not think he started out with any evil or even unethical intentions. I want to believe that the Ponzi scheme of using one bank to pay for a discounted note with another and friends who became bankers just evolved. I believe he loved Rosemary and wanted to keep his lifestyle with his much younger wife intact. It was the ugly side of a life that had been devoted to beauty. That was the contrast that was so hard to accept.

We went back to the apartment after the funeral and had a late-afternoon meal. I don't think anyone had much of an appetite, but we wanted to be together as friends. I planned to leave the next day to go back to New York. I asked Rosemary about the collection from the Musee Cernuschi in Paris. I had spoken to Er-Shih earlier on the phone and had asked when he would take the collection to Mrs. Regenstein in Chicago. He had said to wait four to six weeks.

"Don't you want to insure it?" I had asked. He replied that it would be a waste of money, since all thirty-two scrolls fit into two small, long suitcases. He said he would first bring the collection home, before going to Chicago.

To me, it was quite natural to ask Rosemary if she knew about the collection and where he had stored it, but she said she didn't know anything about it. We looked in the house in Marbella and couldn't find anything. I suggested it might be in her apartment in Lucerne. I changed my plans and flew to Lucerne with Rosemary and her entourage the next day.

We went into the apartment, sat in the living room, and had a cup of tea. "Can we look for the collection?" I asked.

Rosemary said that this was a private affair and that she would look for it herself. "Wait here in the living room," she said, "and we will look around," indicating Er-Shih's daughter.

About an hour later, they came back and said the collection was not there.

It did not make sense. It had to be in one home or the other, and we had been to both, though I had not been allowed to search personally. There had to be an explanation. Either Er-Shih sold the collection to pay his note to the bank or they were lying to me to keep the collection for themselves. One scenario was as bad as the other.

"I'm in the hole for $350,000, which was my 30 percent of the collection," I said. I left the apartment with an uneasy feeling that perhaps Lilly, his daughter, might know more about it than she let on. That sinking feeling in my stomach was growing worse, and the thought that I had been betrayed started eating away at me like a cancer.

"Freddie, you know what a state she is in," Mrs. Vander Mael said. "Leave her alone for the moment. Everything will eventually be cleared up."

A few weeks later, I received a letter, dated May 16, 1972, from Lilly. She again thanked me for everything I had done for the family and her father, and then she asked me not to pursue the search for the scrolls. She said Rosemary had tried to commit suicide shortly after I left Lucerne and suggested that I should beware of doing something that would give me a guilty conscience if anything happened to her.

I flew back to New York and tried to contact Interpol and the world's prominent Chinese art dealers to ask them to notify me if any of the scrolls were put on the market, but the banks had already beat me to it. I had no idea that Er-Shih had been borrowing money from other banks. When a few months went by and nothing turned up, I asked a Swiss lawyer in Lucerne, Dr. Lenhart, to block some of Er-Shih's property against my $350,000 investment. He told me that I was second in line; Chemical Bank was claiming $500,000 for the notes Er-Shih had forged from Mr. Brundage—the same scheme as my notes!

The Only Remaining Mystery

On October 27, 1976, an article appeared in the *New York Law Journal* reporting that Credit Suisse and Chemical Bank were suing each other over the forged Brundage notes. Before his death in 1975, Brundage had denied signing any of the notes in question. After that article appeared, I stopped following the case but did hear that Credit Suisse finally won the suit. I was also in touch with Rosemary's lawyer, Mr. Liebowitz, and an appraiser named Mr. Vangoweng, who was also trying to collect some debts after Er-Shih's death. After the liquidation of Er-Shih's property and art, I received a token settlement of about eight thousand dollars from the estate, or about five cents on the dollar. The only remaining mystery is who in the world is holding thirty-two scrolls from our collection. So far, none have come up for sale, to the best of my knowledge.

During this time, I was in touch with a top expert in Asian art named Vadime Elisseeff, who was also Er-Shih's friend. He claimed that Er-Shih owed him one of the scrolls. Mr. Elisseeff published a beautiful volume with magnificent photographs of Asian art, and he sent me a copy. I called Frank Caro, the gallery owner who had appraised Er-Shih's art before the Paris showing. When I last spoke to him, Mr. Caro was over ninety years old. He remembered Er-Shih, always spoke very highly of him, and claimed that Er-Shih was a knowledgeable Chinese art collector. The gallery does not exist anymore.

Several years after Er-Shih's death, I heard that Rosemary had remarried. Although I tried, I could not find out her new married name or where she lived. Our families had been so close for so long, and the fact that she never attempted to get in touch with me told me that what I feared was probably the truth—her conscience prevented her from facing me. In 1978, her mail was in the care of the Belvedere estate at St. Croix, Virgin Islands. In 1979, I learned from Dr. Lenhart a Swiss lawyer, for the estate, that her new married name was Rosemary Longhi and that she lived in West Redding, Connecticut. He also told me that the Swiss and Chemical Bank had asked Interpol and spread the word to all the dealers in Chinese art, but in all these years nothing has shown up. It remains a mystery. I am sorry that I lost track of Rosemary, even if just to have been able to talk to her once about our memories and find out what really happened to the scrolls—and to the heart of the man who opened my eyes to the world of fine art and Chinese philosophy.

What I do have in place of the money is the memory of so many amazing experiences. I also have several beautiful scrolls that I bought from Er-Shih long before the scrolls from the Paris collection went missing. The scrolls hang on the walls in my den on Long Island, and every time I walk in the room, they remind me of my adventures with Er-Shih. Despite the debt, I bought four of his ancient scrolls from his estate auction at Sotheby's in London. In my house in the Bahamas, I have a beautiful watercolor of Toremolinos that he painted, never imagining at that time that one day he would die and be buried there on the Costa del Sol. The value of Chinese art has increased tremendously in the last thirty years and in great demand by new generation of Chinese collectors.

I recently told Annegret that if Er-Shih were to walk in the room right now, I would probably forgive him for whatever he had done. She looked at me as if I had finally caved in to senility, but down deep inside I think she understood. The friendship had just meant so much and the experiences had so enriched our lives that I could not believe we had been taken for a ride intentionally. And like on other occasions in life, one learns and sometimes pays for the learning lesson. It's just the way things unfolded, and underneath it all was still the love and mutual respect of one struggling man to another, each with a rich past, a beautiful wife, a love of life, and an insatiable desire to squeeze every ounce out of every hour.

Art Gallery at Tennisport

Art continued to swim through all I did. For a while, I supported artists at a gallery I set up at Tennisport in one of our buildings which used to be a restaurant, Prudentis, that had been around for many years before I arrived. Later on, when Prudentis moved out, one of our tennis professionals, Chris Haub one of my teaching pros who was also a painter, talked me into converting the empty restaurant into an art gallery. We would use the space to exhibit the work of local artists who could not afford to exhibit in the city. It was an expensive proposition, but I did it. We had a reporter from the New York *Times* come and take a picture at the opening, and his article ran that Sunday with complimentary comments.

Tennisport supported the gallery for about ten years while the club was doing very well, so I could write off the loss, but the reality was that it was a sideshow on a tennis club complex and not where it needed to be, in the heart of a cosmopolitan community. Foot traffic was insufficient and I ended up using the space to store my own paintings and art. I had accumulated more than I had space to hang, though I always kept the four small tennis prints given to me as a present by Dina Merrill from her place in Palm Beach's Mar-a-Lago along with many other pieces of art for anybody to come and see. One of the few artists who did succeed thanks in part to the gallery on the Tennisport grounds was Czech sculptor Lea Vivot, who was already gaining fame for her distinctive outdoor sculptures in Canada.

I thought back to an incident that occurred when I was a refugee in Frankfurt, playing for pay with hitting partners at the Palmengarten Tennis Club. Visitors were either looking to sell me something or looking for business connections. One of the German old-timers when I was teaching in Frankfurt showed me photocopies of works by at least five old masters. He said he knew where the originals were and had access to the person who had them, and he asked if I could find anybody who would be able to buy them. I told him I didn't have any connections with the right people. It occurred to me later that the paintings could have been stolen from the museums by the German soldiers during the war. I never saw the person again, but through all these many years later, I have kept the photocopies.

Chapter Six:
Successful: Tennis Inc in Armory on 34th St, West Park Racquet Club on 97th St and Columbus Ave, Tennis 59th St Under the bridge, Cedarhurst Tennis Club and the Eminent Domain of Tennisport Inc in Queens

What weighed on my mind more was that while art as hobby was an increasingly consuming interest, my real business was tennis. In 1970, shortly after we hosted the first Virginia Slims tournament with fair prize money for female players, the Thirty-Fourth Street and Park Avenue Armory had been demolished to make way for a new school and office building. I still had my teaching job at the Rockaway Hunting Club, teaching juniors in the summer, and I had private lessons, but now I was renewing my acquaintance with tennis entrepreneurship. I located space on the upper west side at Ninety-Seventh Street and Columbus signed a lease and created the West Park Racquet Club, expanding to eleven outdoor courts. I played with New York City mayor John Lindsay from seven to eight almost every morning. The club was also becoming a popular place for many good tennis players and for celebrated artists and business people as well. Frank Stella, Barbra Streisand, Dustin Hoffman, Robert Redford, George Soros and Jack Dreyfus (of the Dreyfus Fund) Larry Kudlow, Alan Mnuchin (the last two now on President Trump's team) and many other celebrities joined the club. With tennis beginning to boom as a sport and my courts doing so well, I had every confidence that my West Park lease would be extended. I had visions of building several indoor tennis facilities in Manhattan.

After three years, confident of promise by Alcoa agent for a lease extension of 30 years, I applied to the city planning commission to expand on the site by building an indoor tennis court and hired the renowned zoning lawyer, Abe Lindenbaum, to help me. After fighting the community for two years and spending a small fortune, we lost the case. Even my personal acquaintance with the mayor didn't help. He said he did not want to interfere.

At the end of the seventh year, with the lease at the Ninety-Seventh Street club about to expire, I began negotiating for an extension. Just when it looked like the lease would be renewed, my luck unexpectedly changed, and not for the better.

A gentleman walked in saying he would like to play tennis, a reasonable enough request, except he wanted to play then and there, and on that particular day, all the courts were booked. When I informed him of this, he puffed up and confidently retorted, "You'd better find an opening for me because I own the place now. I just bought it!" He responded then introduced himself. "My name is Disk Dean, of Lazard Freres." I said that nobody had advised me and was shocked when he arrogantly answered that "nobody has to".

I had no choice but to take one of the lessons off the schedule and let him play with one of the professionals. Fifteen minutes into the game, we had to call an ambulance because Dean had twisted his ankle. His twisted ankle was the twist that sealed my fate. Somehow, he blamed me for the injury even though he had tripped over his own sneaker. He now owned the land on which he was playing and on which I was dependent for my livelihood. There went my chances of getting an extension of the lease. After waging and losing the battle to build indoor courts, I was about to lose the eleven outdoor courts I had built and developed into a solid business. Lazard Freres leased the property without reimbursing me for building the facility (discrepancy in lease) to somebody else and for a much longer period. I never had a chance to bid.

John McEnroe and Champions

For years, John McEnroe asked me to build a tennis court with the same surface used for the US Open in Flushing Meadows. He wanted it so he and other top players could practice on the same surface before the US Open. After a few years, I gave in and built one at a cost of thirty thousand dollars.

About two months after it was finished, John presented me with a check for thirty thousand dollars. I had never expected to be repaid for building a court at my own club at the request of someone who had been playing tennis with me at various clubs from the time he was a child and whose career I had followed as if he were my own son. But John insisted.

"Freddie, I owe it to you for all the years here spent by me and my family. You did not have to do that, and I appreciate it very much," he said. John was very generous. He even played once with an elderly lady who didn't know who he was and asked him to hit few balls with her. To all the people around in the club it was a surprise when he went and hit with her for at least 15 minutes. He did it few more times during the period of years going on the court to play when asked by people he didn't know. So you see, sometimes the media makes judgments on people without knowing the other side.

Charity Events at Tennisport

Over the years, we held many charity events at Tennisport, including some for Lionel Corporation's sponsorship of the Junior Tennis League and the Fresh Air Fund as well as some for groups raising money for cystic fibrosis and the USTA. In 1986, just before Christmas, we held a charity event for the Vitas Gerulaitis Youth Foundation, featuring exhibition matches with Bjorn Borg, John McEnroe, Peter Fleming, Ilie Nastase, and Gerulaitis himself. Our sponsor, Cacharel, created fantastic decorations.

Elton John and David Frost at my charity Tournament.

Doubles with Kenny Rogers, Bjorn Bork and Marty Raynes.

On another occasion, we had a magnificent Christmas tree in the middle of our building and dinner for twelve hundred people, including Sir Elton John, Mary Tyler Moore, Alan King, Kenny Rogers, and Tom Cruise. The party was a big success. The only disappointment to me was seeing some of the tennis celebrity players

My daughter Andrea giving advice to Vitas Gerulaitis.

using cocaine in the back of my office. That was a big shock. The only souvenir from the tennis exhibition was from Sir Elton John's ankle high shoes and leather jacket with sign on the back of it Hard Rock Café which were forgotten in my office and never picked up after he had changed to tennis shoes. My wife gave away the jacket to one of the Nixdorfs sons Michael, but the shoes I kept in my tennis collections.

The other little memoirs:

Tennisport was also popular among the world's personalities. When Saudi Arabia's Prince Faud visited the United Nations and wanted to play tennis, we had to close an entire building just for him because security was so tight. He had a team of about six security guards, and requested to play with a professional... preferably a woman tennis pro. Later one of them was employed as private tennis teacher in Riyadh, Saudi Arabia. We heard that she did well and was able to open a travel agency in Riyadh.

Also, the Bhutan prince who stayed in N.Y. while his wife was treated for cancer at Sloan Kettering Hospital, gave generously and presented a beautiful gold Bhutanise bracelet as appreciation to our pro, Linda Sigelman, for the improvement of his game. Prince Albert from Monaco was also a regular player and the list goes on which only Doris our manager could remember.

Concorde to Paris for Lunch

I used to play at Tennisport with Nicky Forstmann, whom I had known since he was about twenty years old, when I was a professional at the Rockaway Hunting Club. We became very good friends. Nicky was an extraordinary young athlete and a good person to everyone. He was very successful in his investment business with his brother Teddy, who was occasionally my doubles partner at Rockaway Member and Guest tournaments. We became good friends and Nicky invited us to many of his social events.

Whenever I played with Nicky or some other clients I made it a very close game so he would feel like he would have a chance the next time. One day, soon after I turned sixty, we played on the front tennis court and had a gallery of about fourteen people watching us. Most of them were female because Nicky was a very handsome bachelor at that time. When we finished, we shook hands right in front of the gallery.

"I have more time now, so I will be playing more," Nicky said. "When you turn sixty-five, you won't have a chance!" Our pro David Brent from the gallery said, "Nicky, I would not bet on it."

Nicky turned to me. "I will bet you that I will beat you when you are sixty-five, and the prize will be a trip for you and Annegret and me and my girlfriend on the Concorde to Paris for lunch." I said okay and forgot about it.

Five years later, when I turned sixty-five, David Brent reminded me of the bet, So Nicky and I played, and I won. The next day, by messenger, I received the two tickets. Annegret and I decided to cash the tickets, and we flew economy. Nicky was supposed to have lunch with us in Paris at the famous La Tour d'Argent restaurant, but he did not make it for business reasons.

This was not the only bet I won. When I met Stein Eriksen, the famous Olympic skier, who came to the Coliseum's annual ski shows we used to play occasionally. One day, I invited him to Vasata, the Czech restaurant on Seventy-Fifth Street that had the best duckling in town. We had more drinks than we should have and started getting loud, bragging about our tennis games.

"I can beat you if we take a bottle of Champagne, and every time we change courts, we have a drink," Stein said. "The bet is twenty skiing lessons against twenty tennis lessons." To this day, he still owes me the twenty lessons. It was fun.

Presenting to John McEnroe First Tournament Trophy at Age Ten

Tracy Austin and my son, Freddie

Chris Evert giving lesson to my daughters Daniela and Andrea

Presenting John McEnroe (left) his first trophy, and Gotlieb (right) his runner-up plate.

With the armory demolished and no chance of renewing the lease on Ninety-Seventh Street, I was displaced yet again with no time to spare to find another location. This time I managed the dealings with the Department of Parks and the local community to secure a lease from the city to build a bubble-shaped facility under the Fifty-Ninth Street Bridge. I built eight indoor courts and called it Tennis 59. The lease was once again for seven years but only for the six months a year of cold weather. I began the first Easter Bowl tournament at the Fifty-Ninth Street club. John McEnroe and Tracy Austin played their first tournaments which I co-sponsored with Seana Hamilton, there when they were only ten years old. I have the previous photo of handing to John McEnroe his first trophy and runner up trophy to E. Gotlieb.

After three years of successful operations at Tennis 59, I wanted to build as many tennis courts in the city or surrounding areas as possible. By coincidence, I stumbled upon a real estate auction advertisement. The last property listed, owned by New York City, was out in the Rockaways. I looked at the map and found out that it was very close to Atlantic Beach, and I thought it would be a good place to build a tennis club. I went to the auction and sat in the front row. Most of the properties had already sold, and in time they came to the one I was waiting for. The starting price was ten thousand dollars. I thought maybe I could buy it for thirty to forty thousand. The bidding started, and before I knew it I was bidding fifty, sixty, and seventy thousand. Higher and higher we went until I found myself bidding $120,000. Suddenly, I woke up. I did not have this kind of money. I stopped bidding and was relieved when someone behind me placed a higher bid. When the bidding stopped, I turned around to discover that six rabbis had been bidding on the property. They came to me, saying, "Thank you, sir. You finally stopped bidding! We needed that piece of property to exchange for Yeshiva University."

They were so happy, and I was so relieved. The rabbis wanted the property so they could exchange it with the city for a different property. They needed to give the city a certain amount of acreage for the exchange. For them, this was a great deal. I pass by the area often, and now it has four high-rise apartment buildings on it.

The next morning, I played tennis with New York City Mayor John Lindsay again. "John, you owe me a lot of money," I said jokingly. "If I had not been at that auction, that city property would have been sold for ten thousand dollars." "In the name of the city, thank you!" he said. "And come tonight with Annegret to my party at Gracie Mansion." His parties were always fun and meeting many interesting people from all walks of life.

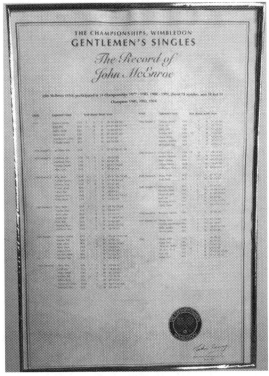

Wimbledon committee presented John McEnroe plaque of his winnings, which John presented to me for my 80th birthday

Cedarhurst Tennis Club and Highway

I found a piece of property owned by the city at the corner of Rockaway Boulevard and Brookville Boulevard. It was a big gamble because a clause in the contract said I could be asked to leave at any time with as little as six months' notice. Since the location was so remote and so close to the JFK Airport, I convinced myself that nothing could happen. I built six indoor courts and six outdoor courts and came up with an idea to help boost interest, especially among women. On the opening day of Cedarhurst Tennis Club, Robert Redford, whom I had taught at West Park Racquet Club and who had become a friend over the years, came and played with some of the new members. It was great publicity that helped make for a successful opening.

As had happened so many times before, the Cedarhurst club, after years of initial success, was the target of misfortune. Five years after we opened, a surveying team from the city pulled up, hauled out their equipment, strode across the courts without saying a word to anyone, and started putting down stakes smack dab in the middle of the tennis courts. I watched at first from my office, stunned, and walked out to find out what was going on. Surely, there was some mistake. No, I was told—no mistake. An extension of the highway was scheduled to be constructed, and part of it was going right through the club. The time frame was three months. I had no choice but to move. Luckily, I managed to break even.

Forty years later, there is still no highway there, and my former Cedarhurst Tennis Club land remains empty, neglected, and abandoned except for the overgrown bush, trash, and debris that now populate the corner.

My property of Tennisport taken away by Eminent Domain and
being developed by the city into a successful housing project

This was happening to me, a man just trying to build more tennis facilities in New York. The seven-year contract with the city for Tennis 59, the bubble under the Fifty-Ninth Street Bridge, was expiring. An entrepreneur with better connections in city hall had managed to obtain the lease to the property and I, who had developed the formerly neglected site into an active neighborhood tennis recreation center that provided youngsters with a place to learn and adults with a place to play, was getting the boot. I was desperate to find a new place. I searched by car, asked my contacts, and even hired a helicopter to fly over the New York area, scouring for a site. I checked rooftops, parks, and vacant lots. I enlisted the help of a real estate agent who called one day to say he had a place he wanted to show me in Long Island City. It was more than a bit of a long shot, he said, but worth taking a look at if I had plenty of imagination.

Tennisport Arial View in 2005

It was in Queens where the New York Daily News had a printing plant on twenty acres at Borden Avenue and Second Street. The realtor and I climbed a thirty-foot high mountain of discarded lumber, scrap metal, old newsprint, and garbage. It was an abysmal eyesore. Once we scrambled and clung to scrap metal and finally reached the top of the three-story heap, the view we saw was breathtaking. New York City, with a direct view of the UN building, was sprawled out before our eyes in a spectacular sight as I had never seen it before. I knew instantly that this was where I would build my new club. Because it was on the East River, people had the option to arrive by boat, and I decided right then and there it would be called Tennisport.

TENNIS ACADEMY TO OPEN THIS JANUARY AT TENNISPORT

Freddie Botur (middle) chats with Senator Jacob Javits and Mike Wallace after a playing lesson.

Senator Jacob Javits, myself and Mike Wallace.

Negotiations began immediately with a gentleman named Arthur Schucht from the *Daily News*. I asked him if I could lease the north part, seven acres, of the property, and he agreed after confirmation from his bosses. The project was huge, but so was the fervor with which I was about to tackle it. We agreed on a twenty-year lease with a renewal option. Even with my good reputation with banks from previous enterprises, I had a hard time raising half a million dollars to begin construction.

Serving tennis balls from a balloon at the opening of Tennisport in 1972.

I began by clearing the huge pile of refuse. For weeks, I worked along with a crew, breaking down that pile of debris, clearing the site, and falling asleep exhausted but exhilarated at night, even though I had yet to secure the necessary financing.

Collapse of experiment with Geodesic dome.

The Mafia Guys

Early on during the club's construction, after we had erected the steel structure of the clubhouse and built the roof, we started to build the outdoor tennis courts. Around ten o'clock one morning, two men came to me wanting to know if the workers who were running the equipment were union people and who their supervisor was. I told them it was none of their business, but they informed me that it was indeed their business and went over to talk to my employees, all of whom suddenly left the site, leaving all the equipment just where it was. After that, the goons came over to me, and one said, "Now you have supervisors." They turned and walked away.

At three o'clock that afternoon, the men returned and demanded three hundred dollars in cash on the spot. Flabbergasted, I told them they had no right to do this.

"That's too bad," one of them said, squeezing my shoulder hard enough to ensure that I got the message. "Tennisport could have been a nice club."

The implication was clear: without the money, the workers would stop work on the job. I had no choice, and I thought that if I paid them, it would all be over. I reached into my pocket and forked over the extortion money they demanded. Then I called on my people to come to work at 6:00 a.m. the following day. Four hours after work began, the same time as the day before, the goons showed up again, and the same thing happened for the next three days. I asked Mayor Lindsay, the labor leader Victor Gotbaum who played several times a week and had complimentary memberships and others if they could help me. Like typical politicians, they said, "I can try."

Nothing happened.

About the fourth day, I went to the Prudentis restaurant our tenant on the property, and sat down to tell owner George Prudentis my story. "Oh, why didn't you come over the first day?" he said in a tone of voice somewhere between sympathetic and just plain syrupy.

He left the restaurant and made a few quick phone calls.

A few hours after I got back to the building site, the Mafia guys left without asking for money and never returned. Of course, I owed George, and I paid up, too. A few years later, the restaurant's rent payments began slowing down. When I asked about it, I was told that business was not that good. Slow rent was followed by no rent. Nine months went by without a penny. I wanted to talk to George myself. I walked into the restaurant one morning and found it cleaned out and empty, without a sign of life or piece of equipment—stripped to the bare wall. It was an expensive thank you for the calls he made.

Despite that little incident, Tennisport was a very successful operation from the day it opened in 1972. By the mid-1980's the club had a membership of twelve hundred. It was big advantage to businessmen who would not have to wait two or three hours in public courts to get court time, our members included corporate leaders. I could not take much time off giving lessons when busy to build up Tennisport, to which some critics were doubtful that it would be a success. Only early in the mornings. I played several times a week at 6 o'clock in the mornings with Rupert Murdoch and at 7 with Ralph Lauren and his wife since none of my pros liked to get up so early in the morning. Tennisport was opened to play at any time. I also had very good and reliable staff. Our members were CEOs of major companies, bankers, shopkeepers, educators, politicians, and celebrities, as well as institutional members such as corporations, schools, the United States Tennis Association, and the Junior League.

Tennisport was doing well enough, in fact, that with my friend Heinz's help, I was able to purchase the property I had started out to lease. It would be the first time I owned the land own underneath the courts I occupied, and despite having been displaced from four other locations, the truth is that I never even thought about purchasing a piece of New York real estate for a tennis club until Heinz made a proposal one day that was hard to resist.

"Why are you leasing this, Freddie?" he asked me. "Buy it." "I don't have enough bank credit yet" I replied.

Heinz soon afterward guaranteed the loan and became fifty-fifty partners on the land only. It was a very good real estate investment for him and me. Located at the front of our property was a large, empty power plant with four huge iron stacks; broken windows; and darkened, soot-covered brick and a restaurant, Prudentis, that was a bank fifty years ago where people would come by boat to cash their checks. It was a modest start, but from that start I created Tennisport— sixteen indoor and fourteen outdoor courts—where the likes of Rod Laver, John McEnroe, Ivan Lendl, Cliff Drysdale, Jim Courier, and other greats played; where Pete Sampras and Arthur Ashe trained when they were in New York; and where New Yorkers from CEOs and celebrities to regular working folks flocked by the hundreds on weekends. They played tennis where the tennis greats played, showered where the tennis greats showered, and shared locker rooms and stories and walked across the parking lot to enjoy the Italian restaurant's homemade fettuccini. I did well enough to pay Heinz back ahead of schedule and with interest in a very short time, and slowly becoming more involved in small real estate projects.

Meanwhile, I was visited by Joe Sarro, the builder who had built clubhouses for me at previous three other tennis locations. "Freddie, there's a beautiful mansion for sale out in Lawrence," he said. "It's dilapidated, but we can fix it up and make some money reselling it."

We did, and Sarro and I began a real estate partnership on an upbeat note, feeling good about being partners in something we felt added to the community and in our interests, all which was providing additional revenue for both of us. With that positive feeling, we learned of an opportunity farther out in Rockaway to build eighteen duplexes lining a street zoned for two-family residences. Sarro said that given the strong market for affordable duplexes, we could produce a good product and make a handsome profit, but it required my investment. I agreed to put in a substantial amount. Again, real estate, which has been the pot of gold at the end of the rainbow for so many immigrants, was going to smack me in the back through no real fault of mine or of my partners.

The city planning department delayed the project for two years, just enough time for the housing market to take the worst dive. It took us six years to sell the duplexes, and in the end, I was lucky to break even. Occasionally, when I am in the Rockaways, I stop by to see "our street," and the houses are still in great shape. We also bought a property in the Hamptons that became quite profitable, but luckily we sold it before Joe, a very good man to the end, passed away.

Skiing and Tennis Connections

Throughout my years at Tennisport, I met not only great tennis players but also world-champion skiers through Karl Plattner, who was the director of the ski school at Hunter Mountain in the Catskills, where we often skied on weekends with our children. He introduced us to Toni Sailer and Egon Zimmerman, both Austrian Olympic gold medal winners, and many others who ended up being guest tennis players at my clubs I guess about 90%of skiers play tennis. On one occasion, Egon, who owned a hotel in Lech, Austria, invited me to go skiing with him there. I had been there before as a guest of Frank Wyman and on other occasions with C. V. Starr at his apartment in the Hotel Post at St. Anton. A few years later, we got spoiled and stayed at the luxurious Hotel Zurserhof in Zurs, where over the years, through skiing and après-skiing, we have met many interesting personalities from different parts of the world.

Rich Girl, Unfortunate Love

On one of our ski trips to Zurs, Austria we met a young couple from Pittsburgh named Julia and Bill. They liked our company because we knew everybody there and they were visiting for the first time. Of course Annegret blond and Julia dark hair two beautiful women in après ski parties were center of attention One of my friends, a great skier and former champion named Andre Papp, was one of the resort's ski instructors and taught Julia and her husband full time during their vacations. And it happened just like in some storybook, Julia fell in love with him. Who could have predicted it? Julia and Bill looked like a happy couple with four children. Julia was a tall beautiful woman and was admired by anyone who met her. Knowing she was married, Andre, a true gentleman, told us that he didn't want to get involved with her and went out of his way to keep his distance while we were there. At the time Annegret and I left, we didn't know what would happen later.

By the next summer, everything seemed to be okay. We were invited to Julia and Bill's place in Pittsburgh and went to a few parties with them. We have never been in Pittsburgh before, it was interesting being introduced to a different type of society than in N.Y. It was then that I found out Julia was the heiress to a large industrial company. A few months later, she called us to say that she would be in New York's St. Regis Hotel and invited us to the theater and dinner. She had also invited a few more friends. Her mother called day before and asked me to rent a bus that would serve cocktails and appetizers while driving around town to show her guests downtown before going to the theater.

After the theater we all went to the 21 Club for dinner. The evening was a great success, and even Julia's mother loved every moment of it. The next day I received a beautiful present from her, a pair of gold and diamond Tiffany's cuff links that I still treasure to this day.

Julia asked when we would be going skiing again. We said February but that we would be going a few days early to go to Munich for the Fasching Beer Festival. Julia asked us if they could join us. We stayed in Munich for two days and had a good time. From Munich, we went to Zurserhof ski resort in Zurs. It was there we found out that she had been after Andre the whole time, and it was then that her husband decided to leave her.

It seemed to me that she was a very spoiled woman. She followed Andre everywhere even though he still refused to have an affair with her. Andre told us that she followed him to Mexico and threatened to jump out of a window if he did not return her love. We didn't hear from them since. A few years later, I received a letter from Bill's lawyer asking me to testify in his divorce proceedings. Bill claimed that I was the one who had introduced Julia to Andre, and he blamed me for the divorce. It was so ridiculous that I didn't even answer the letter. I never heard from them again.

It was rumored that Julia's mother thought her daughter had psychological problems and moved with her to an island they owned in Florida. With the help of a friend, an archbishop, Bill and Julia tried to put their marriage back together. A few years later, I heard that Julia had died, possibly a suicide. Not long after this, Andre became depressed and committed suicide himself, in Sydney, Australia. What an unfortunate story. Andre was a wonderful, very sweet young man.

Acapulco, Mexico

It was not the only story in our newly married life with a dark ending. We met many other couples on our tennis or ski trips. I think that partially our language ability and Annegret's charm and myself being a very good skier, we also met Carlos and Helen and their two children on one of the many ski trips in Austrian the Alps. We became friendly with them and they often came to visit us in New York, and we would visit them in Acapulco, Mexico, where his business manufactured and supplied cement for the entire west coast of Mexico.

Carlos had invited us to his place in Acapulco after we had our first two children. His house was on the top of a hill overlooking Acapulco with walls leaning one hundred and fifty feet high against the hill because, in this area, owners had to protect their houses against landslides. His main dining room looked like a Chinese pagoda, and the house's roof was made of copper.

At the time of our visits, and unbeknownst to us, kidnappings in Mexico had started to become daily events. On our last visit, Carlos posted two guards with machine guns at the gates and explained the need for them. We drove past them and enjoyed our stay over the next few days, though I could not help but wonder how, if there were an attempted kidnapping, a kidnapper would know if the children were Carlos' or mine.

One evening during dinner, at a table set beautifully with fine china and crystal, shots rang out. Pellets hitting the copper roof sounded almost like hard rain.

"What is this, Carlos?" I asked.

"Oh, this is just a friendly monthly reminder," he said. "When my neighbor down below gets drunk, he starts to shoot at me, reminding me that he hates me!"

"What do you do?" I said.

Carlos just continued eating his dessert as if this were nothing out of the ordinary. We all just sat there while bullets hit the roof. Finally, Carlos stopped eating, wiped his mouth with a napkin, and said, "Let's go."

He brought down his shotgun. We went to the edge of the wall, and he shot a few rounds at his neighbor's roof. There was peace again. It looked to me like their monthly ritual.

Dinner with the Seibels' was an adventure of its own kind. One night, I found an appetizer on my plate that seemed to be moving. It turned out that the moving creatures were live eels, a specialty being served in our honor. "Just squeeze lemon on them," Carlos advised. "It numbs them, and then you can swallow them." I did not manage this, and neither did Annegret, although she bravely tried. Another time, for breakfast, he gave us turtle eggs. They looked like Ping-Pong balls with shells as hard as plastic.

Helen was an incredibly beautiful woman, and it was evident that Carlos was very much in love with her. She was quite young when she was diagnosed with breast cancer, and despite being treated at the Memorial Sloan-Kettering Cancer Center in New York for over a year, she died. As a widower, Carlos was totally distraught. He could not overcome his grief. He stopped working and turned the business over to his son. He was very proud that his son ran the business so well.

One day I got a sad phone call telling me that Carlos' son had been murdered. The young man had gone with his girlfriend on a ride in Acapulco. They stopped at the roadside to kiss, and they were attacked by two armed men. Carlos' son tried to protect his girlfriend from being raped, and the bandits shot him.

Carlos was a wealthy businessman who had contacts and influence in government. He offered a substantial reward for his son's killers, and the two guys were caught and convicted. They were both policemen from Acapulco. They were sentenced to thirty-three years in prison, but Carlos was not satisfied. Every month, he paid the people who run the prison handsomely to have the men raped every single day. I do not know how long they survived, but that was his revenge. He sold his business and never went back to Mexico. We communicate once in a while. I know he found another love and just hope he is happy.

Nicky Forstmann: "If You Can Afford it, so can I."

About six months later, I called Ron and asked him if they had any bids on the ranch. I had let my hopes soar, already picturing myself and my family on the ranch, the improvements we would make, and the wide open spaces we would enjoy. When he said it had sold for the asking price, my heart sank. Three months later, the property was on the market again because the buyers had wanted to pay only a nominal deposit and asked the bank to take the rest in notes, but the bank wanted the ranch off its books for cash. Ron called me. I upped my offer and said that was it and I wasn't going any higher. Again, the offer was rejected, but by this time the idea of the ranch had wrapped itself around me, and I knew I had to find a way to finance it. Certainly, the price was right.

One afternoon at Tennisport, I was sitting on a barstool having a cup of coffee when my friend Nicky Forstmann came off the tennis court, perspiring, red in the face, and tired. He asked for a Coke, and a brilliant idea struck me like a lightning.

"How about a partnership on a ranch, Nicky?" I asked.

He looked me straight in the face and said, "We have known each other for at least twenty years, and you would not do something that would not make money. If you can afford it, I can too."

We shook hands. He did not ask how much the ranch cost or even where it was. He just said, "It's a deal."

A week later, we purchased the ranch. Nicky, the same man who had bet me the flight on the Concorde and lunch in Paris, sent me a check for 50 percent of the total price of the ranch property and became a partner without ever seeing anything or signing any papers until closing when he finally did see the ranch with his beautiful fiancée, Lana. He was extremely happy with the purchase even after receiving a speeding ticket just about a half a mile from the entrance. The sheriff looked into the car and upon seeing two beautiful blondes, asked; "Are these your women?" which we found hilarious. Nicky was an ideal partner, fast and decisive.

Ron became our consultant, as promised, and Ken Fear, the former owner, became our manager.

In notes, but the bank wanted the ranch off its books for cash. Ron called me. I upped my offer and said that was it and I wasn't going any higher. Again, the offer was rejected, but by this time the idea of the ranch had wrapped itself around me, and I knew I had to find a way to finance it. Certainly, the price was right.

One afternoon at Tennisport, I was sitting on a barstool having a cup of coffee when my friend Nicky Forstmann came off the tennis court, perspiring, red in the face, and tired. He asked for a Coke, and a brilliant idea struck me like a lightning.

"How about a partnership on a ranch, Nicky?" I asked.

He looked me straight in the face and said, "We have known each other for at least twenty years, and you would not do something that would not make money. If you can afford it, I can too."

We shook hands. He did not ask how much the ranch cost or even where it was. He just said, "It's a deal."

Tennis Pro and Cattle Rancher

*Annegret's visit to Jackson Hole in 1962 with
her uncle from South Carolina*

When I first started at Tennisport, one of my very loyal members was a gentleman named Ron Saypol, the president of the Lionel Corporation and a few other enterprises. Even though Ron was a bit heavy, he enjoyed tennis and played three or four mornings a week from seven to nine. Ron also supported the sport, running several junior tournaments sponsored by his corporation.

During one conversation with Ron, I happened to mention that I was planning a camping trip to Jackson Hole with my family that summer, so he invited us to visit him there. A friendly and generous man, Ron took us to a mountaintop to fish in a beautiful Alpine lake called Sleeping Indian. He was extraordinarily thoughtful, and we had a great time with him in Wyoming.

About four years later, the Lionel Corporation went out of business, and poor Ron, once so generous and filled with the joy of life, was left with no more than the shirt on his back. He lost his home and everything he had. Utterly and completely broke, his wife left him and he had to take care of their two children. Ron decided to move permanently to Wyoming, where he had friends. He went to work for a real estate company and introduced to me few deals during a one-year period that wound up being profitable for both of us. I was glad we had remained friends, and I was happy that he had earned some profit from real estate transactions. About two years later, he called me up one morning and said, "Freddie, can you do me a favor? I had two clients from New York who were supposed to buy Cottonwood Ranches in Sublett County Wyoming which was in default. They just cancelled on me. The bankers are already flying in from Denver to meet them. I feel very embarrassed by this. Could you act like a buyer?" I told Ron that I had never even been on a real ranch before. "Just act like a buyer," he replied.

The bankers arrived, and we drove over an hour south in the direction of Pinedale and then onto Daniel Junction. From there, we went about nine more miles to the entrance of the ranch. With the exception of visiting a dude ranch with the children and the Nixdorfs a few times, I had never in my entire life been on a real ranch like this. Picture me acting like a wealthy New Yorker driving with bankers and the former owner of the ranch (who was now the manager) in a Suburban. What I saw was only a mound of sagebrush, squirrels, and endless dust. After about thirty minutes of driving through the middle of the ranch, I simply looked around and asked how far away the ranch's boundaries were. I was bored, tired, and restless. "Let's go back," I said. "I have seen enough, and you want too much for it."

"Mr. Botur, you are not even halfway through," one of the bankers said. "Do you see those mountains? That's where the ranch ends." As it turned out, the property was approximately twenty-five miles long and four miles wide.

On our way back to Jackson Hole, the car was silent. Finally, the bankers asked me to at least make an offer on the property. *Now*, I thought, *I am really in a pickle*. I gave them the first answer that came to mind.

Mountain Man parade in Pinedale, Wyoming, 2010

Freddie Botur Jr. serving steaks on the Ranch.

Our guest on the Ranch, Patrick,
found a moose head skeleton

Being honored as UNCLE SAM
in the parade on 4th of July 2005
at the Lawrence Beach Club

Freddie Jr., myself, my wife, and my daughters Andrea

and Daniela on an outing at the Ranch, 2000.

My Son Freddie Jr. received prize for Environmental Ranching

"It looks like the Sahara Desert."

But I did not want to put Ron, who had suffered enough losses in his life and had helped me make money, in a negative light, so, knowing I had some cash available from selling the stock I had in Heinz's computer company, I made a very low offer.

"Now we know you are definitely not interested," one banker said. Ron saved face, and I was clearly out of any danger that the offer might be accepted.

The price they were asking then was three times what I offered. Thinking about it at home the next day, the possibility of one person owning so much land bothered me. I knew I had read something on the topic, of ranch ownerships and I went to research it. I found an article, attributed to "The Dwamish Chief, Sealth (Seattle)" after a search:

How Can You Buy or Sell the Earth?

The Great Chief in Washington sends word that he wishes to buy our land. The Great Chief also sends us words of friendship and good will. This is kind of him, since we know he has little need of our friendship in return. But we will consider your offer.

If we agree, it will be secure the reservation you have promised. There, perhaps we may live out our brief days as we wish.

When the last red man has vanished from the earth, and his memory is only the shadow of a cloud moving across the prairie, these shores and forests will still hold the spirits of my people. For they love this earth as a newborn loves its mother's heartbeat. So, if we sell our land, love it as we cared for it. Hold in your mind the memory of the land as it is when you take it. And preserve it for your children, and love it........ as God loves us all. One thing we know. Our God is the same God. This earth is precious to him. Even the white man cannot be exempt from the common destiny. We may be brothers after all.

While I shared the Indian belief that ownership is an anathema and our common destiny on Earth binds us, I couldn't stop thinking about this land. It was beginning to grow on me unexpectedly, like a woman you meet and can't get out of your mind. I decided to visit the ranch again. I met the manager and drove with him all the way through. Over the next four months, I made the trip five times. I started to see the ranch with different eyes. I became interested in the way of ranching life there, out in the middle of nowhere. The manager and former owner, Ken Fear, fueled my interest more when he revealed the history of the ranch and the people who made it what it was. On one of our tours, I told Ken that if ever I bought it, I would expect him to run it just like it was his own.

Before shipping

The first four years, we were lucky as cattle prices were high. We made some money and with the help of my wife and son, we started to repair and rebuild the original homestead settlements.

With only five months a year of good weather to work in, the project took about ten years to complete.

The land grew on us, and we felt like we had always owned it. Nicky felt the same way, though he visited infrequently.

Nicki was spending most of his time with his fiancé, Lana Wolkonsky, whom he later married. Lana was a professional pianist who had won a major prize playing Chopin in Warsaw at the age of eighteen. She has also published several books of poetry. When she visited us in Jackson Hole for my birthday in 1997, she gave me a poem she had written in my honor, called:

"Your America"

In your honor sport has done......
The graceful court, the gentle
stroke of racquet, now of club
A like in hosted, welcome days,
Many visit, play their game and
'Round your polished hearth do
share a warm, a friendly talk.

Away beyond our mighty heights,
Another land you made your own
Lies frozen in the winter months;
Then reaches for the birth of calves
As fields become a picture so alive
In fragrant beauty. When you walk
The hills and climb with pride, this
Land is your America..... your favored
Slope, your kindled joy by fire's
Radiant glow. These the nights with
Endless stars, as many fond of you
Become.... Received well a virtue
Had: your name outlasts us all!
The smile you shine, its giving
Soft, remind us of another land

Once left behind: your mother-earth
Which gave you soul and so has
Touched us all in heart, in years.

As the years have gone by, our ranch has become what in Czechoslovakia we call a "Domov" in Czech and "Heimat," in German. This is hard to translate, but it means something like "a home where you were born and to which you feel much attached." I am very happy that my son Freddie Jr. decided to run the ranch after taking a year off from school. He has a good grasp on the complex operations, has improved the land, its irrigation, conservation values and the cattle operation. I am very proud of him.

A lot of heart and money has gone into restoring the ranch's homesteads, honoring the integrity of their original structures that were built when the first settlers came. I often wondered how people lasted through such harsh winters without heat and the conveniences we enjoy today. Later, we encountered other challenges unrelated to the physical infrastructure and makeup struck, mostly economic, but we were fortunate to survive. Many of the small ranches did not survive, and many ranchers were forced to sell their land to large corporations. Luckily there are people with the means to be able to buy these ranches, which started to be non-economical for the original ranchers and aren't able to keep them in original western style and don't have to sub- divide them.

The way to go, in Wyoming

As I mentioned above a lot of old timer ranchers, because of the cost of maintenance and shortage of cowboys were sold. The buyers usually are well to do people or large cattle companies who could carry their losses or write them off. Our friend rancher and neighbor, Jack Swabacher was a legend in Wyoming and real cowboy. He was also surrounded by a lot of friends who were full of life and humor. One of his best friends, Paul Von Gundhard, when Jack passed away arranged a vigil at his house, Paul said to his friends who came in to pay their respect "Jack would like to have at least a last party to send him off" so Paul and his friends took him out from the mortuary, brought him home then dressed him up, put him in a chair so he looked as if he was still alive, they all drank to him and tried to pretend that they were sharing jokes and stories with him while all having a good time. One of the stories when Jack got married for the second time on the ranch with a minister, Paul Von Gundhard and couple of his friends interrupted the wedding by riding the horses and shooting their guns in the air, saying that he cannot get married unless they said it was ok. The stories showed you the real way of life in the many parts of the west which you wouldn't read about, this kept the cowboys happy.

Cowboys, a Dying Breed

The ranching business is changing nowadays because working cowboys are a dying breed and are becoming harder and harder to find. Even hiring on a temporary basis is getting tough. When you need students or young people to help with haying or other odd jobs, the ranch cannot afford their wages, because the oil and gas companies in the neighborhood pay three or four times more than the rancher can. We are lucky that my son Freddie, who manages the ranch, has found a very reliable foreman who is also a rancher, Saul Bencomo. Saul is a natural cowboy and is one of Wyoming's top rodeo ropers. Before Saul, we had T. J. Simmonds, one of the cowboys whose family was riding horses like you would see the old cowboy movie also tamed wild horses, so we count ourselves among the fortunate.

We also have on a part-time basis, my friend Patrik Strilka, from my old Czech neighborhood. Patrik enjoys the beauty of the mountainous surroundings of the ranch and can tell stories back at home. He purchased a lot for his family at a reasonable price. Our ranch has beautiful views, good fishing, good hunting, good hiking, and a lot of wildlife, but just like some of the other ranchers with similar problems, we continuously feel pressured to make up for the losses by subdividing and selling parts. Instead, my son has made favorable conservation arrangements with local Land Trusts in the State of Wyoming, which pleases all those concerned.

cowboys, a dying breed.

Cottonwood Ranch, round up.

Over the years, part of the pleasure of the ranch has been for many friends who have come to visit, exploring the countryside along with us on foot, on horseback, or by jeep.

"You think I don't know how to drive?"

One of those occasions almost changed our lives. A very close friend and neighbor from Cedarhurst, Long Island, showed up along with his wife and son, much to our delight, in 1992.

We took advantage of the beautiful summer weather, showing them around Yellowstone National Park, going rafting on the Snake River, taking long walks, and hiking the mountains. One day during the visit, Dick asked to go exploring. He wanted to see the entire ranch. It was a particularly glorious day, about seventy-five degrees under blue, blue skies. I was driving my Chevy Suburban, showing them the beauty of the country, pointing out the old cabins, and talking about how the settlers lived. About three o'clock in the afternoon, Andrew said he wanted to do a bit of fishing, so we headed back. As I went to climb into the SUV,

Dick looked at that vast expanse of open land and asked to drive. I didn't feel comfortable about it for some reason and told him so.

"What do you think—I don't know how to drive?" he challenged me.

Not wanting to offend him, I stifled my objection and went around to the passenger's seat, concerned, but reluctant to insult my friend. I comforted myself with the knowledge that with almost no traffic on the ranch, little harm could befall us. Two miles into the ride with Dick going too fast, I begged him to slow down. I rarely put a seat belt while driving on the ranch, but some providence from somewhere was looking after me that very minute and I clicked the belt into place. Instead of slowing down, the car sped up. We were at the top of the hill, going too fast downhill. Dick finally applied the brakes, not realizing that the pebbles on the road act like ball bearings. Downhill we went, and then we traveled another quarter mile straightaway. As we came close to the crossroads, we saw two cows standing in the middle of the road. He slammed on the brakes again, but with the pebbles, the SUV spun, hit the side of the road, and rolled three times, the roof crumpling like a wadded-up paper envelope, landing with the wheels up and spinning. Andrew was in the back seat screaming, and I was able to crack the door open enough to roll out. Dick couldn't get out. He was trapped inside and unable to move. All of our equipment—guns, food, and radios—were on the hill. I started to look for my cell phone. Of course, I didn't realize that I was bleeding profusely from the legs and shoulders and had a sharp pain in my ribs. Luckily a car passed by, and the driver called the ambulance on his cell, but the ambulance was forty-five minutes away in Big Piney. While the driver knew who I was and called my son, who was only about ten minutes away, running the cattle, he sped to the scene in his truck, bearing tools and equipment he normally carried for repairs around the ranch. After a struggle, he and another cowboy who was with him were able to get Dick out of the car. When the ambulance arrived and loaded us onto stretchers, my son wanted to ride with us. I absolutely refused and told him to go back to work, not realizing what bad shape I was in or that I was in shock.

This pic speaks for itself

It was an hour before we got to the small emergency room. A doctor who must have weighed at least three hundred pounds and, given the region, was probably a veterinarian, stitched up our wounds temporarily, enough to get us by ambulance to a hospital. By then it was nearing seven o'clock, three and a half hours after the accident. The same ambulance drove us to the hospital in Jackson Hole an hour later, where Annegret and Priscilla, Dick's wife, were waiting. Dick's injury was much more serious than mine, and to this day, he walks with his neck bent forward. I had broken every rib on my right side, suffered some lacerations on my legs, and had back pain. Since then, I have chronic difficulty with and pain in my legs.

A few years later, I was diagnosed with a pancreatic inflammation which we didn't know if it had any connection with the car accident. Thankfully I have been successfully treated by Dr. Larry Werther in New York. How would I know that nearly twenty years later, I would have a knee transplant followed by another accident? And yet I can walk with a cane and see without glasses at the age of ninety as I commit my memories to paper. Dick has included the accident in his own book, *Mr. Canada*. When we meet now, over dinner or for another social occasion, we talk of all sorts of things, but neither of us ever mentions that day.

The accident marred our summer and scarred Dick for life, but it did little to dampen our growing affection for the ranch or our feeling of being at home in Wyoming. Still, we could not ignore the incumbent economic reality. After making money for the first four years and investing all of it back into the property, making repairs and improving the infrastructure, we started to lose money. Nicky and Lana were very busy socially and had started a family, so they visited the ranch only a few times. Then, Nicky, a heavy smoker in the past, died from lung cancer at the very young age of fifty-two. Since Lana did not want to have any real interest in the ranch, I had to buy her out. After Nicky's death, she became reclusive for a long time. It took her a very long time to recover the joy of life she once felt, but she has mended in recent years. Now when she comes to visit, she brings her children to go skiing and visit us over the Christmas holidays. We continue to welcome her as family.

When I reached eighty, I could suddenly hardly walk and had to give up tennis and skiing. At the Mayo Clinic, Dr. S. Dyck diagnosed me with a degenerative nerve disorder called Charcot-Marie Tooth disease and predicted I would be in a wheelchair in two or three years. It was devastating news for me and after consulting with Dr. Werther, he advised that I be transferred to Mount Sinai Hospital in New York.

Stem Cells

My very good friend, Herbert with whom I had been playing tennis and had shared many stories from the past visiting weekends for almost thirty years, had shown his generosity and sent his plane to transfer me to New York. Since then, I have been trying to slow down the process by using different types of stem cell treatments successfully.

One day in The Bahamas while I was swimming in the ocean, a few feet away from me a gentleman turned his head and asked, "Aren't you Freddie Botur?" I said "yes". He said, "Do you remember me?" I said, "No". Then he said, "I am Henry Nordhoff. We played tennis thirty years ago at Tennisport when I was working for Pfizer Corporation". So, after the swim, we sat down on the bench and reminisced on the good times at Tennisport. He noticed that I had difficulties with my legs, so I explained it to him that I had Charcot-Marie Tooth disease and there is no cure for it. He told me he became the Chairman of the Gen-Probe Stem Cell Institute in San Diego and would inquire about what could be done. I started to go once per year to receive stem cell treatment with Dr. Bayer. It does not cure my leg problem but it helps to support the rest of my joints and keeps me healthy.

My daughter Daniela managing Jackson Hole Hitching
Post Lodge (Later sold to the hospital)

A Family Matter

In the 1990s, my daughter Andrea after finishing New York University was offered a job in television working for the well-known news anchor Chuck Scarborough. Within a few weeks, Andrea decided that it would be more comfortable for her to work for her father since she was good tennis player. She, who had grown up around Tennisport, grew into a management role there. It was a perfect fit. One day, Andrea got married to a golf professional and they had two children. Six years later Andrea has divorced and has happily remarried few years later. During Tennisport's heyday, Andrea decided to open a golf range named Golfport on vacant property behind the club. It was a good idea, but it just didn't take off. After two years of Andrea's best efforts, she gave up and closed it down, and she decided to devote more time to her children.

My other daughter, Daniela, who graduated from the University of Colorado decided to take cooking school first in Paris and then in San Francisco. After that, it seemed to be a natural to take the opportunity for me to buy the Jackson Hole Hitching Post Lodge Motel to start business on her own. A few months later while learning the Spanish language in Cuernavaca she called me and said, "I am in love and am going to get married and settle in Mexico." Years later, after her divorce, she moved back with her three wonderful children to Jackson Hole and is taking care of them. Because of the violence and kidnappings in her area it made our family very nervous, so we were happy to have them back in Wyoming. One of our well-liked teachers was John Cosme who had a vision for Tennis T.V being the future of the sport.

In Praise of My Teaching Pros

I could list hundreds of celebrities and personalities whom I have to know through my tennis clubs, from Robert Redford to Barbra Streisand and from New York's mayor to Arabian princes.

The ones that would rank highest are those who work in the industry, making it possible for those who enjoy the sport of tennis to play when they want. When they want on courts that are well maintained and with rackets that are well strung. The teaching pros and coaches are the unsung heroes of the sport; they are so critical to its survival that there ought to be a whole separate book in praise of pros.

It's been said that some of the business world's biggest deals are made on the golf course, and I don't disagree, but I'd be ready to bet that many important connections are also made on the tennis court benches and are launching pad for career opportunities just like it happened to me.

Teddy Forstmann, one of the founders of the private equity firm Forstmann Little & Co. and the global sports management and media company IMG, assisted several pros, in the business. Forstmann also hired away one of our better pros, Suad Rizvanbegovic, who became one of his closest friends joining him in the insurance business and found great success. Because of Teddy's generosity, Suad convinced Teddy to give Twenty Million Dollars to Croatian Hospitals according to Suad After that Suad retired and became very friendly with Croatian President Tudman and because of that also became the chairman of many Croatian sport associations. Another pro, Ron Glickman, became a successful stockbroker and still occasionally plays with George Soros. An Australian pro at Tennisport named David Brent became a partner in a tennis club in Cedarhurst. Bill Talberts son Peter taught for several seasons and many other pros who worked in the summertime to support their studies and who went on to become doctors or lawyers, Marian Gangler was very popular teacher for some personalities like Jack Dryfuss or Tom Brokaw while studying Theology, some of the pros still teaching part time in the Hamptons on Long Island.

During my more than fifty years in the tennis business, I employed teaching professionals from all over the world. Doris our manager figured out that during my 50 years in New York I must have had at least one hundred teaching pros employed. Many of them are now retired and have stopped playing, but they keep in touch.

Skip Hartman (chairman of the New Your Junior League and big tennis entrepreneur) worked as my assistant at the River Club for a few summers in the late 1950's to earn money to support himself at Princeton University. Today, he is the number one tennis promoter for public parks and public tennis facilities in all of New York. There are so many skills that go into making a successful tennis environment or assisting a great tennis player. But perhaps none is more vital than the often-overlooked "Stringer".

A good stringer is vital in the tennis world, and another successful employee, Roman, who learned stringing skills at our Doris Sterling Tennis Shop became so proficient at the trade that he now strings rackets for the world's most famous tennis players. Another of my pupils, John Reese, a one-time Wimbledon qualifier, later became chairman at the Newport Tennis Hall of Fame and Museum. In 2009, when he was being inducted, the outgoing chairman said Reese's "loyalty has been key to our efforts to preserve the past and inspire the future of tennis."

Finding students is, I have to confess, a lot easier, because they find you. Finding good pros, who not only play a great game of tennis, but have the magic touch in teaching by encouraging others and helping them develop their strengths. There are no headhunters, so Annegret and I would often partially plan a vacation around a visit to potential candidates. I recall an incident that occurred shortly after the first time we met and interviewed Suad Rizvanbegovic for a teaching job, and also son of my very good friend from Ostrava, Karel Vita, who wanted to come to the USA and work for us. Unfortunately, Vitas son had an eye defect and after I explained to him the employment situation, he decided that he would be better off at home in Ostrava. Annegret and I travelled to Vienna, scheduling a side trip to meet with another young man as he was son of my close friend. We were staying at Vienna's famed Grand Hotel, which lived up to its name. We met Suad, who drove all the way from Zagreb and who applied for the position explaining the difficulties in Croatia. After the first interview with another candidate I offered him the job at Tennisport. He was very happy that I accepted him, and with that piece of business behind us, Annegret and I decided to rent a car and visit vineyards in the nearby town of Grinzing, north of Vienna, known for fine white wines and also home cooking.

We had the afternoon free and were in high spirits when we took off for unknown territory. As dusk fell, we realized that we needed to find our way back, especially after having a few glasses of wine. This was long before the days of GPS. Like most of the male species I believed that I could drive my way to a destination without having to ask for directions, as if doing so could prove once again my mental prowess. Dusk turned to darkness, and we were truly lost. We had heard stories about motorcycle gangs, but neither of us wanted to say out loud what we feared inside. Straight ahead was a gang of eight men on Harley Davidson motorcycles staring down at rental car with lost tourists. It looked like something from a movie set that makes you think you can go ahead and change the channel now because you know the outcome and don't want to see it. I gathered up my courage, rose to my full six-foot frame, and boldly asked if they knew the directions to the hotel. The young man I asked paused and then went back to the group, and they talked among themselves. My heart was racing. I just knew this was going to end badly and no one would find our bodies for days, maybe weeks. The man strode back, looking even larger than before. "We will take you there," he said. I began to breathe again. Annegret, who always has faith in people, looked up at me as if to say, *See? I told you so. People are really good.* They led the way. We were all of about fifteen minutes from town, and when we got to the entrance of the hotel, I was so grateful that I told them to park their bikes in front of the hotel and come in to the lounge for a drink on me. The doorman was aghast. "They cannot come in here, sir," he said in his most officious voice, as if their very presence was a personal affront to him. I still felt a little upbeat from the wine, looked him squarely in the eye and said calmly, "Do you see that there are eight of them and one of you?" I motioned for the men in leather jackets to follow me into the hotel bar, and we had a great time. When the manager stopped by, he complimented them on their manners and welcomed them to the Grand with an ironic smile. Although I chuckle at the picture we made in that elegant bar, with a gang of eight in leather and less-than-perfect grooming, thinking of them always reminds me of how it's sometimes easy to misjudge situations.

TENNISPORT Dreams crashed

As Tennisport became better established, I tried to encourage developers and hoteliers to build a hotel on our property in the late 70th. Jay Pritzker, Hilton Hotels, Canadian Pacific, Howard Johnsons, and a few others considered combining the tennis club with a hotel on the river with a Hydrofoil connection to Manhattan. But timing was not in our favor. During the 1980s, when Tennisport was climbing in popularity, interest rates, too, were soaring, hitting 22 percent and holding. No one was building. The plans were shelved.

At one point, I proposed to Heinz Nixdorf that we should build an apartment building on one of the parcels. We engaged Harry Green and Ron Ogur, architects, to start the process of planning and designing the building. Harry and Ron presented plans and arranged to meet with the city planning commission. They wrangled with the community for several years to get the permits just like Abe Lindenbaum for us on West Park Racquet Club.

At one point, we seemed to reach a compromise: the city agreed to approve the zoning if the bottom portion of the building could be used for commercial uses. Although we argued that nobody would be interested in using the space for business at that time, city officials said they would find commercial tenants within six months. Six months elapsed, then another six months, then another, and still nothing.

It turns out that whatever we planned would become irrelevant. It looked like we were purposely stalled by a higher government power.

1992 Eminent Domain, End of a Dream

In 1992, a crowd of two hundred officials including New York Governor Mario Cuomo, New Jersey Governor Mario Cuomo, New Jersey Governor Tom Kean, New York City Mayor Ed Koch and many other high ranking City and State Government Officials, gathered on our Tennis courts for a grand announcement and ceremony—they were taking my Tennisport. They were condemning our property, which was decorated in red, white, and blue for the occasion. Under the right of eminent domain, they were going to demolish the club and build a low-cost, multiuse high-rise apartment and retail building.

Paying Rent to city for my own property

We hired the best condemnation lawyers at the recommendation of our member lawyer I. Leimas's firm, Goldstein Brothers, who specialize in eminent domain cases. But it was to no avail. We lost the case in 2003.

Ironic during the years the city allowed us to stay on a six month notice rent. Tennisport enriched their coffers, paying $500,000 a year in rent for the right to stay on our own property that they were seizing even as we fought for fair market value.

I came with my daughter and the lawyer to the Supreme Court in Brooklyn for the hearing. Already, when we walked in the dark courtroom and seeing the four older women judges who, to me, looked like they were out of a nineteenth century Russian movie... very unfriendly and gloomy-looking, and while my lawyer was presenting my case, one of them looked at him with a smirky expression. So this was already an indication of the future decision (Some of my friends who had been following our struggle mentioned the possibility of underground forces to get the property).

Below is a letter from my lawyer, John Haughton from

Goldstein brothers, said to be the best Eminent Domain specialists on the unjustified final ruling of the value of the Eminent Domain:

If one looks towards the Queens waterfront and just south of the iconic "Pepsi Cola" sign, you will see the Tennisport property. It is one of the world's most recognized shorelines, with a prominent spot on the western shore [sic] of the East River. The property is diagonally across from the United Nations Building, with a clear view of the Empire State building, the No. 7 subway train is just two blocks away and it takes only one stop and five minutes to reach Grand Central. The area around Tennisport has seen the construction of seven residential buildings, over 2,600 apartments and over 120,000 square feet of retail.

Pursuant to the power of eminent domain, on February 25, 2002 the Queens West Development Corporation ("QWDC") acquired title to the Tennisport property. The purpose of the condemnation was to facilitate QWDC's Hunters Point (a/k/a Queens West) Waterfront Development Land Use and Improvement Plan.

On May 20, 2009, the City of New York Economic Development Corporation acquired the subject property from QWDC and then transferred title to the City of New York.

In order to determine how much Tennisport should be paid for its property, a trial was held before the lower court on various dates in February through April, 2013.

Both Tennisport and the City agreed that it was likely that the Tennisport property would be rezoned for residential use. The area itself was severely underutilized and with a shortage of waterfront land, it is logical to conclude that the City would welcome development to maximize its use. Moreover with the decreasing availability of affordable housing in the City, residential development would be an attractive alternative.

In valuing the property, Tennisport proposed that the property be developed with a multi-story residential development, encompassed by three buildings and five residential towers, two of which would contain commercial and residential space, as well as, open-air parking for residents and shoppers. The total square foot area of the proposed building was 2,024,088 feet. In *valuing this development site, Appellants' appraiser relied upon 13 comparable sales of residentially and commercially zoned property in Queens, Brooklyn and Manhattan. He arrived at a value of $55 per developable square foot, for a total value of $85,000,000.00.*

The City claimed that, even though the property would likely be rezoned, it should be valued as a big box development site, i.e., auto supply stores, stationary stores, drug stores and hardware stores. Based upon ten big box sales, the City contended that the fair market value of the subject property was $45 per square foot of land area, for a total value of $13,440,000.

In a terrible decision, the trial court said that residential development was not economically viable. It valued Tennisport as a big box development site and awarded it the amount of $59.86 per square foot of land area, which equaled $18,086,658.

Just one look at the Queens Waterfront shows that the trial decision was incorrect. In choosing to discard residential development, the lower court cited not to facts but to broad, unsupported generalizations. **For example, it found that the subject property could not attract residential tenants because "the neighborhood is even less appealing in the Winter, when the sunsets [sic] before five p.m."** *The sun sets at the same time in every neighborhood in New York City, whether residential or otherwise, and that has not seemed to deter any of the city's 8.4 million residents from living here, nor any developers from building buildings here.* **Yet, the time of the sun set in winter was inexplicably a part of the trial court's rationale.**

In fact, almost every basis that the trial court relied on was either contradicted by the evidence at trial or not supported by any evidence at all. The trial judge also penalized Tennisport for the fact that the City prevented anyone for rezoning or developing this area due to the impending condemnation. The City stagnated this area and kept it frozen in time as underutilized industrial land and then the trial court ruled against Tennisport because the neighborhood was filled with underutilized industrial land.

Tennisport appealed, but was unsuccessful.

Despite the fact that the area is filled with high-rise residential buildings, the Appellate Court adopted the trial court's decision that high-rise residential was not economically viable. We suspect that, in part, this decision was made because the Appellate Court did not want to invest the time or effort to actually consider the evidence. And, also in part, because the court is often loathe to award owners large sums when those payments are being borne by the taxpayer, irrespective of whether or not the claim has merit.

Tennis 'love' lost

33-year-old club closing in Queens

By TOM TOPOUSIS

For Tennisport — one of the city's best-known public recreation facilities — it's game, set, match.

After 33 years in Hunters Point, Queens, the center that has hosted celebs and tennis stars will be shutting its doors July 31 as the city begins work on a massive housing complex overlooking the East River.

"We'd love to stay another year, but the city is telling us they're ready to put a shovel in the ground," said Andrea Botur, whose father, Freddie, built the club on the site of an old dump in an abandoned section of waterfront.

For three decades, the club has been a labor of love for the family.

The 16 red-clay indoor courts and eight remaining

JOHN McENROE
Built own court at center.

Har-Tru outdoor courts have played host to Tom Brokaw, Robert Redford, Sean Connery and Liam Neeson, among others.

John McEnroe liked the place so much, he built his own court there.

For the past 20 years, the Boturs have known match point was near.

First, the state had eyed it as part of its enormous Queens West development. In 2002, the state forced the family to sell the property through eminent domain.

The Boturs negotiated several two-year extensions while development plans went bust.

Finally, the city bought the property from the state in 2006.

Mayor Bloomberg has proposed building 5,000 units of middle-income housing and a school for the 24-acre site.

City officials said they would begin work preparing the land, which has little infrastructure, by the end of the year.

Freddie Botur, a tennis impresario of sorts, had opened and been forced to leave a series of tennis clubs around the city be-

fore he landed at Hunters Point, then an industrial wasteland just one subway stop from Manhattan.

"It was a garbage dump when my father found it," said Andrea Botur, whose dad is now 87 and still works at the club.

"It seemed courageous at the time. He built the club and thought he was safe here."

One of the club's charms is its seeming timelessness. For the past 20 years, Botur has operated under the threat of being forced out. His daughter said that as a result, they never really changed the place much.

"A lot of people like that," she said of the '70s style that remains.

Now the Boturs are busy finding new jobs for their 30 employees and 15 tennis pros.

tom.topousis@nypost.com

Newspaper article

*Being evicted by eminent domain signed by
three governors and the mayor*

*My daughter, Andrea, and the Mayor of Bloomberg
discussing condemnation about her Tennisport.*

Promises for Tennisport replacement.

We fought them for many years, they have taken our Tennisport. They have taken part of my soul. But they also have not paid the fair market value for the beautiful prime property. They have not and cannot pay for the lives they have interrupted and the value of business and appreciated value of our seven acres river view of prime real estate property. I had a vision when nobody wanted it. It took my vision and courage to open the door on the other side of the East River and city took it unjustly after I developed the finest tennis facility in New York. It set my goal fifty years back.

You see, it was one thing to watch young pros come and go as they moved on to new lives with our blessings. We nearly always kept in touch and remained friends. But it was another thing to say good-bye to people who had been with us for most of their adult lives and were now left without jobs because the government was taking Tennisport from under their feet and displacing them, some thirty-two people in all. Pablo, my tennis court builder and supervisor, had been with me for forty years. Doris, who spent thirty-eight years with us, went and opened her own tennis shop in Huntington, Long Island. After twenty-five years with us, Miriam Porto opened Madeira, a Cuban restaurant, in Long Island City. Doris and Miriam had been the backbone of Tennisport. But in the end, I was forced to walk away. I could not bear to turn around and look back. My daughter Andrea, who was my right hand in running the club, cleaned out my office. As I said in the beginning, I am one-sighted: forward. There were so many persons of influence and players and pros who went to bat for us, including Bernie Mendik the real estate mogul who knew all the top officials including Mayor Bloomberg. John McEnroe and Virginia Wade personally said, in his words on DVD tape which my daughter Andrea did for our 35 Tennisport anniversary:

John McEnroe's Comment:

"Ask anyone who knows anything about tennis in New York City, and you will get appreciative words about Freddie Botur and his clubs. I first laid my eyes on Freddie probably way back when I was playing the Easter Bowl as a teenager. Freddie was under the Fifty- Ninth Street Bridge. At that time, you would learn the history and tradition of this sport and get an appreciation for what our sport is all about. You really don't make much of it at the time; you don't realize the people that will impact you later on. The people that really care about this sport—those people are few and far between. Freddie has been here for probably fifty years and more in this New York area. He is really like an icon for our sport."

Virginia Wade's Comment:

And one-time top female player Wimbledon winner and many other fop tournaments Virginia Wade, who played at Tennisport regularly, said:

"I remember coming here to Tennisport—one of the first years of coming here to the States and thinking what an amazing place it was, with New York on the other side. I was a young kid who was just beginning a tour, and already Freddie was a presence, and then Freddie became one of these characters that was larger than life. He was this good-looking guy with this accent; he was sort of like a tennis purist. He loved the game so much, everything he did was to enhance the game of tennis."

Jim Courier's Comment:

Jim Courier called me the "great poobah of tennis." I'm not sure what that means, but I don't think it was powerful enough to stop New York from taking what I had built, though I owe him a thank you for being so generous with his compliment.

Allan Tessler's Comment:

The former Senior Managing Partner of Shea and Gould, a long-time member and close friend of our family in Wyoming, who was involved with David Markin (who was involved in building new tennis stadium in Flushing Meadow and USDA has honored him by putting the plaque in the stadium) could not believe the obstacles of my case until Allan personally met with my lawyers the Goldstein Brothers to hear their view on the case with hopes that we will win the case. I was very thankful that he took his time and confirmed to me the difficulties which lay ahead of us.

*From our trip to India and Bhutan, with Allan and Francis
Tessler, trying to forget the loss of Tennisport in 2009.*

The former USTA president David Markin, with whom Allan
and I played very often serious tennis matches, asked USTA for
support said to me, to abandon the fight. "You are a rancher now,
Freddie," he said. His words stung. I don't think he meant to hurt;
I think he just wanted me to enjoy what years I had left without
spending them waging a war he felt I could not win. Yet I believe
that we will win. In the end, after all we live in democratic country.
I will never get Tennisport back, I know that now even I was
promised part of the property to replace more south of us as they
show it to me on the picture, we agreed but they reneged on it. I
hope to get a fair price for the condemnation to build another tennis
facility, if we find another place. My battle will help pave the way
for others who put their hearts and souls into creating something
good only to have it snatched from them without respect.

Ironic – Tennisport Praha (Czech Republic) compared to Tennisport N.Y.

I find this predicament personally ironic. When the Communists took over my parents' business, they nationalized a piece of our real estate in a suburb of Prague on which my father had planned to build a subsidiary of our business from Ostrava. Fifty years later, I have gotten my father's property back from the Czech government and have considered building tennis courts there. It is called Tennisport Praha. The president of the company is Dr. M. Urbanova, who used to work for me at Tennisport in New York during the summers in order to earn money so she could afford to study to become a doctor. She has successfully succeeded and practices in Prague.

When I opened Tennisport N.Y. in 1972, it never occurred to me that a similar situation could happen in democratic America. The only difference in America was: the city and state didn't take the property without paying for it. The Communists took the property and kept it without paying anything for it as they had done to my father. The prime Tennisport property has to be paid for its full real estate value. When I took it over there was a thirty-foot tall heap of discarded newspapers and lumber yard trash. We cleared it and made a big improvement in the area.

The pain goes beyond business. It is personal, and it hurts. After spending over fifty years building the tennis business in New York, being ousted from one location after another by city or for other uses for the properties that I had improved, this final condemnation is especially painful to lose our tennis future in New York. My daughter Andrea and I had considered finding a new location where school children, tennis leagues, and thousands of tennis players could enjoy a healthy, wholesome, nonviolent sport, but I am now ninety and the dream of starting over is beginning to fade. I take serenity from this work of verbal art about the real meaning of land ownership and take great pleasure in knowing that I spent a life doing what I loved surrounded by people who shared the pleasure.

Investment in Azerbaijan

As a member of the prestigious Lyford Cay Club, I have made many friends, one of them being Hanelore whom Annegret and I met through my oldest friend in the United States, Frank Wyman. Hanelore's son Peter, while studying at a university in New Jersey, was often a guest in our house in Long Island and a friend to our children. During one of my visits at Lyford, Hanelore came to me and said, "You are Czech, and I would like you to meet a very nice, young, bright Czech who is interested in buying my house by the name of Viktor Kozeny for dinner." After I met Viktor, I started to play tennis with him and his wife Ludka, and his guests occasionally. At that time, he was riding high in the society of the club. He had a good reputation, and his motto was "There's nothing you cannot buy for money." He was admired and was also well connected with very prominent and wealthy people in for a short time. I found out that he made his money from the privatization of Czech industries while buying government coupons from the individual people. Coupons were issued to the Czech population in the amount of a thousand crowns each, and he promised a tenfold return to the people who didn't know what to do with the coupons. They sold them to Viktor's corporation, and most of them got their tenfold return. This way, he was able to amass approximately twenty percent of all of the coupons in the Czech Republic, and with them he was able to buy many profitable industries in the country.

I remember one day seeing the front cover of *Time* Magazine with Viktor's picture and the headline read "Pirates of Prague." The article was neither negative nor positive. At that time, after the Velvet Revolution in the Czech Republic, there were no new rules on regulations in the banking and finance industry, and not many foreign investors were sure of Czech politics. Viktor was able to take advantage of the loopholes and move all of his assets to different countries, hidden in secret accounts, according to the newspapers.

Of course, later on, the Czech government changed the law,

and people started to investigate whether he had done anything wrong. According to Viktor, he was also able to help finance the leading political party during the election of the president. It was exciting at that time to be his friend. Everybody was looking for favors from him, including the Lyford Cay Club when it was selling lifetime memberships. He married when he was young and studied at Harvard University, and then got divorced. Later, he got married to his secretary, Ludka, and had two lovely daughters with her. Annegret and I were invited to their great wedding at the Metropolitan Club in New York.

There, I met his grandfather, who used to be a general in the Czech military during the Communist era. He told me on one occasion that he had been the only privileged person from the Czech government to watch the test of the Russian's first atomic bomb. He commented on how primitively all the guests were shielded from the radiation. It was interesting to listen to him about it.

When the club built a new school, Viktor donated substantial amount to it. I had an opportunity to fly with him once on his private plane to New York, which was a great treat. He has been brilliant in his way of dealing with finances. To raise funds, he used to throw unbelievably elaborate parties; one of them was in Aspen, Colorado, where he had one of the nicest houses to entertain in. Approximately, two hundred prominent people from the banking industry and Wall Street were invited. One of the guests at the party David Koch, who was a member of my Tennisport in N,Y came to me and said, "Freddie, who is Viktor?" I do not remember exactly how I answered but he was not impressed, by him and he left the party early. It was obvious to me that at that time, that David didn't like Viktor and his opulent party. The caterers to be able to have so many people, had to put a floor over the swimming pool. The main entertainers were Natalie Cole and an orchestra. I cannot remember what food was served, but Viktor's parties always had the best of the best. It didn't show at that time but he started to have difficulties with the privatization of the oil industry in Azerbaijan. That's why he was entertaining more—to raise funds, which he did. A few months later, it was all over the newspapers that Viktor and one of his friends had eaten dinner in one of the most expensive restaurants in London and that he had ordered two bottles of wine costing two thousand pounds each.

This was the beginning of the end, because it put some of the investors on alert. Viktor already had problems with the son of President Azerbaijani Alyev, to whom allegedly Viktor had paid a lot of money to be able to buy an oil company named Succor with the Azerbaijani vouchers, which were similar to the coupons of the Czech Republic system. I myself had made a small investment with Viktor. I played tennis at Tennisport with US minority leader George Mitchell, who had supposedly been very supportive of it, he is a very good player and I enjoyed the game. I didn't think I could go wrong and had almost begged for Viktor to take my small amount, as he was looking for a minimum initial investment of $5 million which I could not afford. The moment it was known that president Alyev did not give him the concessions, his biggest investor, AIG, asked for its money back, claiming that he had overcharged the company and the values and it opened door to the rest of the investors to sue him. Since then he has become a headline in many newspapers and magazines.

Before Azerbaijan

*Playing with Czech President, Vaclav Klaus, and President
of the World Bank, Sir James Wolfensohn.*

At the beginning of the new democratic regime, Viktor was buying different industries in the Czech Republic. He visited me one day at Tennisport and asked me if I wanted to make a good commission on a brewery in Pilsen called Pilsner Urquell, the most famous beer in the world. He gave me a large file with all the information and said it could be bought for about $50 million and I could get commission. I was so excited, that I tried to offer it to a few investment

*Senator George Mitchell,
as guest of somebody.*

229

companies thru my club connections, but had no success because it was just after the Velvet Revolution and nobody felt confident what would happen in the former Communist country.

On one of Viktor's visits asked me to introduce him to the president of the World Bank, Sir James Wolfensohn, because he knew that I played tennis with him often and that he had been my neighbor in Jackson Hole, Wyoming. I didn't see anything wrong with that, so the next time I played tennis with Jim, I called up Viktor and told him that he could have lunch with us after our game. I think the lunch didn't last longer than about half an hour because Jim, as president of the World Bank, was very busy and he just wanted to do me a favor by seeing Viktor.

A few years later, when it was known that Viktor had failed to obtain the oil concessions, many of the victims tried to bring him to justice for misrepresenting the price of the vouchers. Viktor's legal defense team tried to get various people involved, even James Wolfensohn, saying that his World Bank had recommended the project, which was completely false. Jim had kept copies of the letters that he had sent to Viktor, and they indicated that he didn't want anything to do with Viktor's project. Of course, all of this was sensational news for the media, which dragged it out for many months.

The situation put a strain on my friendship with Jim, and I felt guilty for introducing him to Viktor. It took a couple of years and many depositions in favor of Jim before the story eventually died. We are still friends and see each other occasionally in Jackson Hole.

Viktor lives in Nassau at Lyford Cay because The Bahamas don't have an extradition treaty with the United States. The district attorney of New York, Robert Morgenthau, tried for a few years to take him to court in the United States, mainly for bribery and money laundering, and almost succeeded, but Viktor—with the best British lawyers from London—managed to keep him in The Bahamas. At one point, Morgenthau was so close that the Bahamian government said it would hold Viktor in jail until the

American government gathered sufficient proof of his guilt. Viktor stayed in Her Majesty's Prison in Nassau for eighteen months.

During that time, his mother when she was not in residence, my friend Patrick Strilka from the Czech Republic, who was visiting me and helping Viktor out part time in Lyford with repairs in his house, would take food for Viktor to jail from local restaurants every day. Victor was lucky that he was alone in a special security cell. I accompanied Patrick on one of his food runs so I could visit Viktor. I think we were the only two visiting males; at least sixty women were visiting their jailed husbands at the same time. It was quite an experience for me, seeing all the pain and sorrow in the faces of the women. We took numbers and had to wait quite a while before ours came up, and then we were driven by bus through more security stations. When we arrived to the main entrance to the jail, prison guards began accompanying us to see Viktor. It's amazing that he survived one and a half years in there.

At the beginning of 2010, Viktor was exonerated on the US charges, and therefore he could not be sent to court in New York. Over the last few years since, he has had to pay his British lawyers a tremendous amount of money.

According to the *Times*, he defrauded investors on the Azerbaijan project for 250 million euros. I am sure there are many other claims, so he cannot leave his golden cage in The Bahamas. While he was in jail, he could not prove that he owned any property in The Bahamas, so he could not put up enough money for bail. He lives in Lyford Cay, a very lonely but good life, and he still cannot travel. There are still some suits pending against him in the Czech Republic so his legal trouble may drag on until the limits of the charges against him have expired. What a waste of the brilliant mind of this young man who could have been a brilliant financial expert in his native Czech Republic. We hope that he and his family will recover from his legal difficulties. I also hope that, one of these days, he will receive a pardon from the Czech president.

FREDDIE BOTUR

Some Interesting Events During the Tennis Years

As I have been going down my memory lane, it has been very difficult to pick which of the adventures and events in my life I should choose to mention. Some of my friends might be offended that I have not mentioned them in the memoirs. Some of them were very personal and intimate friends, and a lot of them are still around and keeping in touch, and we'll see each other once a while. To make a short list of few of the friends in the past whom I met is difficult. But time goes by so fast. Another friend who was waiting and urging me to start my manuscript was a very famous producer and my tennis friend for thirty years, Sam Cohen. Tennisport was a second home to him, but now he too has passed away, as have Nicky Forstmann, Vlasta Koubek, and many other friends.

On some events, one cannot remember all the details. At one point at the beginning of my career at the River Club, a gentleman by the name of Johnson, whose wife was the club champion for many years, manufactured guns with office in New Haven had a patent on a design. (I still have a gun he designed, and a book with the note which he gave to me as a gift.) One of the Moroccan persons (who called the French occupiers "dogs") was very friendly with Johnson, asked me if I could secure the delivery of two hundred of Johnson's guns to Morocco. I probably could have found the necessary connections, but I was a greenhorn in transactions like that, so after a few seconds of consideration, I said that I couldn't do it. It's amazing that, with all the connections I gained throughout my life, I probably could have gone a different direction in my life if I was more experienced in business, and it may have been the wrong way.

So far I am still enjoying life and my family and friends and trying to be healthy. I don't think about the future so much anymore, because it is unpredictable. Every day when I turn on the television and see the news, very seldom do I hear anything cheerful or optimistic and cannot keep up with the pace. The media shifts its attention so quickly, and the pace is part of the global way of life that changes from day to day.

I just finished reading the biography of Sir James Wolfenson, titled *Global Life*. When he lived in Sydney, he was eighteen years old, and I only arrived there in 1950 at the age of twenty-eight, reminds me of another coincidence in my life. Bill Denson, Robert Rosenthal, and I lived very close to one another in Nuremberg but we never knew each other until we met in the United States and became very good friends. Also, I met Koubek, Kozeny, Capek, Holecek, Lendl, and a few others Czechs from different parts of globe after many years in New York. This is how circumstances in my tennis career worked—meeting very interesting people at various points along the way in six decades. Much of that is thanks to my first two jobs in the States—the first at the River Club and the second at the Rockaway Hunting Club, where at that time only top CEOs and presidents of top Wall Street corporations and banks were members. Meeting and socializing after tennis they were part of my learning process related to the financial and cultural way of life in the United States, and I was hungry to learn.

WEDDING AT CHANTILLY CASTLE, PARIS

One of my other exciting stories happened when one of my longtime Tennisport member of Freddie's Angels group, which was founded by Mrs. Howard Johnson and few of her friends, who were well known in social circles around the world. One of these lovely ladies included Princess Jasmin Aga Khan, who also became a good friend since she knew I used to ski and play tennis with her brother, Karim Khan. She had invited my family of four to her wedding at her brother's castle about a half hour from Paris. It was a great honor to be one of the three hundred guests. We flew to Paris, and there I rented a car. I had the instructions on how to get to the castle, but on the way, one of my daughters suddenly said she had a run in her pantyhose. So we stopped on the side of the highway with cars passing by, and Annegret and my other daughter had to hold up a blanket while she was changing. We finally arrived in beautiful part of the Chantilly Castle where the wedding was taking place. We have been introduced to many interesting people from different cultures and personalities, after few hours one could not remember the first one. For my daughters, it felt like a fairy tale, especially being introduced to Begum Salima Aga Khan.

Jasmin was getting married to wealthy Greek shipping magnate Basil Embiricos. We met many interesting people at that wedding, but it is difficult nowadays to remember the details. My daughters, however, will never forget it, especially because they each received a beautiful watch as a wedding memento. After the wedding, we continued our visit in Paris for a few days before returning to New York. We still occasionally keep in touch with Jasmin, who has since remarried and now lives in Park City, Utah, and New York. She lives in the same great ski area as Stein Eriksen, with whom I have very often battled on the tennis court during his visits to New York.

I didn't visit my uncle Charles at the time of the wedding in Paris because of the past disappointments, but he would have been astonished that the little boy from Mistek had been invited to join in events by so many celebrities in his lifetime and I am thankful for his help in 1949.

Joe L. and Buying Soccer Team Slavia Praha

During my tennis career, I had many opportunities to get into adventures other than those involving tennis. One of these happened in Lyford Cay when a friend of mine Renato (husband of Hanelore) who was an enthusiastic tennis player asked me to join him to play doubles on Joes tennis court adjacent to the club. Since then, I have played with Joe and his friends regularly and I made it for them enjoyable keeping the sets very close. On one occasion, Joe said with a smile, "I have a couple of young "Turks" from London who need a lesson." Since I was a left-handed tennis player, he asked me to start to play with my right hand. The guys thought that were no match for them. As Joe predicted, they immediately took the bait and asked Joe for a thousand dollar bet. I had great fun letting them win the first game, and then I switched to my left hand. Joe got great satisfaction out of the result and laughed his head off.

I did not realize at the time that one of the young "Turks," was in charge of managing several European football teams that Joe owned, and one of those teams later was Slavia Praha for which transaction to buy the team I was responsible.

It happened during conversation about football when Joe asked me if one could to purchase the number one or two of Czech teams. At that time Sparta number one was just sold to Slovakia. I was asked how about number two? I contacted friend in Prag Ivan Chadima who had all the connections there to buy the Slavia team for Joe. After many obstacles and at the end promising to build new stadium we succeeded to buy certificates from old members. After about 10 years of struggle to improve the team without success, Slavia was finally sold with reasonable profit.

Annegret and I became good friends with Joe's family and have been invited on many of his adventurous trips. We flew on his private plane to Tahiti, where he had his large boat waiting, to cruise around the islands. We had an opportunity to watch the natives diving for pearls or watching dozens of sharks waiting at the inlet for their prey.

Then Joe invited some of the local Tahitians for party on his boat. I never forget when one of them, the local postmaster said: all my life watching the big luxury boats from the far away I was dreaming how interior of big boat looks like and it happened thanks to Mr. Joe. And what a party it was when the Tahitians danced their native dances, it was unforgettable.

Joes visit to our ranch in Wyoming gave inspiration to look for ideal location for his own paradise of nature and he found it in Argentina. He and Jane and his family have always been wonderful friends and hosts.

Fergie

Joe's house was always full of guests, and on one occasion, Bill and Nancy had been visiting. One sunny afternoon, the three of us and I drove out of the gate of his house to play tennis, and just as we were leaving the gate, Joe saw another golf cart approaching and stopped and waving his hand saying "Hello",we saw a soaking wet lady driving the cart with another friend. Joe, who was in the front of the cart, turned to us, smiled, and said, "There comes Duchess of Windsor, Fergie." Bill thought it was a joke, took one look, and exclaimed, "If this is Fergie, introduce me as the Duke of Marlborough!" We all laughed when we saw clearly that it really was Fergie. The next night, we all had a wonderful dinner at Jane and Joe's house, and Fergie was very natural and fun to be with.

On another occasion, Joe asked us to join him for a few days on the boat around the Caribbean Islands. I said, "I am sorry, but I have a guest, a beautiful Chinese lady friend from New York and Hong Kong."

We have known Doreen and her Husband for quite a few years, when they lived in New York and have been members of our club. We have grown very fond of each other and we have been their guest in Hong Kong several times. I mentioned it to Joe, so he said without hesitation to bring her along. As it happened, Doreen was a very good backgammon and card player in which Joe always enjoyed competition. We had a wonderful time.

In one conversation, Annegret complained about me purchasing my neighbor's property in Jackson Hole. Doreen overheard the conversation and said, "It must be a beautiful mountainous place Freddie, and if you like it as you have described it I will buy it." She had never been to Wyoming and did not know anything about the area, but she trusted my judgment. Months later, I transferred the contract to her, because it borders with my property. Doreen and her son and daughter and their friends enjoy the beauty of the Jackson Hole area and often come skiing. On our travels to Hong Kong, she has always been a most gracious host, and we keep in touch to this day.

Dr. Renee Richards disqualified at US Open

Another of my tennis celebrities at the time of my first tennis club, the West Park Racquet Club, was a very talented young man who ranked among the first ten juniors and used to train with our teaching pros Dick Ruskin. He used to come with his father, Dr. David Ruskin, who watched him and babysat for his son while he was playing. Dick was a very handsome, good-looking man, so it never would have occurred to me that his hormones were turning him into a woman. Years later I read in the newspapers that he went through an operation to physically become a woman. Afterward, she, who started going by the name Dr. Renee Richards became a celebrity because her story was in all the newspapers almost every day. She became very controversial in 1976 when she entered the ladies singles at the US Open and was told she would be refused unless she submitted to chromosomal testing.

It took her quite a few years to get to a normal way of life, still is playing tennis and golf. She also became a successful coach to Martina Navratilova and a few others. She became a very famous ophthalmologist, friend and regular player at Tennisport, and a great supporter of our actions against the eminent domain claim.

Recognition November 16, 2006

At the Hyatt Hotel, the Junior Tennis League awarded me the Twenty-First Annual Civic Leadership Award at a luncheon for four hundred people somehow connected with tennis. Thanks to my former assistant at the River Club and long-time friend Skip Hartman, it was attended by many of my old pupils and friends, including a big surprise, one of my first students from the River Club in late 50th Ms. Walters-Thompson, who was very famous during WWII and known as Rosie the Riveter who represented the American women who worked in factories during World War 2. I was very honored when Mayor Dinkins gave me a golden apple pin as an acknowledgment of my services to the community. The master of ceremonies was CBS news anchor Maurice Dubois, and one of the main speakers was Virginia Wade. Finally, I felt very good about spending so many years trying to promote tennis in New York as I mentioned in previous pages. After all of those years, finally, somebody appreciated my efforts to keep tennis going in New York.

In all the years when I became a refugee and traveled in so many countries, learning and experiencing many other events in my life in or out of tennis activities. It is very difficult to remember sometimes all the details of short stories but I mention some of them anyway like:

Husband and Wife Memberships

During the beginning of the Woman's Liberation Movement, I had just opened Tennisport Club in Long Island City. My membership brochure contained husband and wife membership which was less than single membership. One day while I was at the desk, two ladies approached me and asked for a husband and wife membership. I was very much surprised and didn't want to offend anyone so I asked them to show me the IRS report that they filed together then I will give you the husband and wife membership. But refusing it I was taken to the courts for almost a year at very high expense and lost the case. I guess it was the test case for Gloria Steinman who was at the time the leader of the Women's Liberation Movement. There was no sense in going further to appeal and since then I changed all the brochures to single memberships.

Being a Bus Driver

On one of my trips on Delta from Frankfurt in the sixties, New York airport was under a big snow storm, after circling for a few hours we landed at Stewart Airport near Poughkeepsie, the airline sent us on a bus that would take us to Idelwild Airport, after about fifteen minutes of sliding on the highway missing a few other cars on the way, the driver being very nervous suddenly stopped and left the bus, we waited on him for a half an hour but he did not return. Most of the passengers were Germans, fortunately I was the only passenger who could speak both German and English, it was clear that he stopped near his home, at that time there were no cellular phones and no other way to contact the airport. Since I was the only one who had an American driver's license, I sat behind the wheel and drove it to Idelwild Airport to arrival area, all passengers picked up their luggage from the bus and went on their way. I then called my wife Annegret from the phone booth to pick me up, she could hardly believe that I drove the bus all the way to the airport without an accident. I left the bus at the arrival terminal and no one even noticed or inquired about the bus driver. When you are young you have courage to do things like that, I don't think I would ever do that today.

Club Championship Reward

I became popular and in lot of demand by members of The River Club in NYC, I was booked almost every day on the average of six hours. One of my students who came four times a week for an hour for many years was Dr. J. Marquise Converse. He was a very enthusiastic tennis player and he wanted to win a club championship so we practiced very diligently for about four years and finally he made the finals. Dr. Converse was a very famous plastic surgeon at that time in the sixties, for restoring French Presidents daughter's face after the plane crash. Margie my first wife at one point needed plastic surgery. We could not afford it, but after playing with the doctor for so many years and finally got him in the finals. He did the operation and as a reward for me it was no charge. It shows also how I was respected and well treated by all the Americans I met already at the beginning of my career.

My Wife, Ahead of the Chinese Boom

On our honeymoon in 1965, since we had discount tickets from PAN AM to travel around the world we stopped in Hong Kong and after having few dinners with some of my AIU friends we were hopping from store to store, discovering very inexpensive dresses and suits and shoes. Annegret was very excited when she discovered in one of the stores beautifully styled ladies sandals. She thought the sandals would be a great hit in New York because the sales person offered them wholesale for a dollar per pair. She ordered ten thousand pair and told them the sizes and colors that should be delivered to my new tennis club which was Tennis Incorporated on 34th street. The shipment was supposed to be delivered within three months but was delivered six months later. What a surprise when the boxes arrived, as we didn't realize that the sandals wouldn't be in individual boxes. They came in bulk, mixed sizes and colors. It took a week and five friends to sort the colors and sizes. In other words it was a disaster but looking back it was also fun to see Annegret in shoe business.

Teaching Son of a Cowboy Russian

Our head cowboy on the Cottonwood Ranches was TJ Simmonds who was very well known for taming wild horses and also had a short role as a cowboy in Roy Rogers movie. He and his wife and three children lived in the trailer in the middle of the ranch, next to Annegret's little cottage. The children helped rounding up the cattle, they all rode horses. Actually Billy Jo, his 5 year old daughter, could ride on a horse standing up. We were very fond of the family. To his oldest boy Sean, I tried to explain the way of life during the lonely evenings in the middle of ranch about Czech Republic. There was no radio or television on the ranch, but he was a good listener, at one point he asked me if I could teach him few Russian words, so occasionally I did and gave him also few small Russian English books.

His father, TJ, after being with us for ten years, had a very good offer to become manager in Montana. Few years later, I found out that Sean enrolled in the army and continued his Russian language.

In 2007, he called me up that he was just for few hours in Jackson Hole, he told me that he had been married and had a house in Washington and had a good job as a Communications person for the Government. He had been assigned on Vice President Dick Cheney's plane and just arrived in Jackson. I did not ask him for details about his job. He thanked me for starting him the Russian language which he continued and helped him to career in Washington. I didn't hear from him since then until recently when his father called me and said that he committed suicide. What a waste of a young life.

Charleston Plantation Tennis Court

One of my good members of the Rockaway Hunting Club was Dr. Dominic, he moved in the late sixties to Charleston S.C. One day I got a phone call from him, that he needed desperately my help to advise him what to do, with his tennis court. He invited me and Annegret for that reason to look and advise him. We arrived on a beautiful day to Charleston, and at the arrivals was waiting for us was a Rolls Royce with a driver in uniform and white gloves. On our way to the place we drove through the rows of trees which was full of hanging moss, this looked very mysterious and beautiful. I asked the driver what his name was and he replied Mr. Snow, I asked how come, he said that on the day he was born it was the first time it was snowing in Charleston.

When we arrived to a beautiful old plantation style building we were greeted by Dr. and Mrs. Dominic. I thought I should go ahead and have a look right away at his tennis court, but he said, it was too late in the day, he accommodate us to a very old fashion high ceiling bedroom, you could almost played indoor tennis in there. After that we had dinner, in the dining room, while there I could imagine how the plantation owners who lived there a hundred years ago, had all their slave laborers, with the candle lighting in the House it appeared almost scary. The next day in the morning after breakfast, I again asked about the tennis court, Dr. Dominic replied, first you will have to see my Moth and Butterfly collections. He then took us about three hundred feet from the main house where there had been long narrow buildings, we spent a few hours being explained about his passion of collecting the different species of these moths and butterflies, there must have been thousands of them.

Finally we went to the tennis court with his manager and there I was looking at about 4x4 piece of grass, sticking out of bitumol tennis court, then he said, "this is my problem" they advised me to replace the whole court, so I told them that it wasn't necessary and showed the manager how to repair it. Later in the day Mr. Snow drove us back to the airport.

I used to play tennis

One of the members of the RHC, who was very good golfer decided to play tennis again after twenty years in the eighties. He booked a lesson with me, bought new racket and six grass court balls. Five minutes later, after hitting them over the fence, he went to the tennis court post and broke the racket in two pieces and walked away angry. He came back few days later and again after about ten minutes broke the racket and said he will never play again. He eventually played a few years later. This was the strangest tennis pupil I had. He just didn't have the patience and I didn't mind sales of two new rackets to him.

And few other tennis stories (many of them I can't remember anymore)

Oleg Cassini, well known designer for Jackie Kennedy, was a very good friend and tennis player who used to come at least three times a week to play with one of my Pros. After the game we used to have lunch. He was a great animal lover and had on his farm in Oyster Bay on Long Island, where he rescued all kinds of animals that are abandoned and kept them there. He was the center of attention when he always ordered two hamburgers for my German Shepherds at our table. The dogs already knew when he parked his car in the parking lot and always ran to meet him wagging their tails.

Then there was another extreme dog lover, a publisher who use to "take-out order" of two steaks, which he claimed to bring to his dogs.

Then there was another gentleman, Boris Kliot, with a Russian background who not only loved tennis but also gypsy music, once he asked me to get the Gypsy Orchestra from the Paris night club Rasputin, to celebrate his Seventy birthday at our Tennisport. That was one of the finest parties Tennisport ever had.

Another gentlemen from Europe who was short of cash asked me to buy his 160 acres property in suburb of Bakersfield, California. I bought it with the idea of building a tennis complex like the one in New York and I called it also Bakersfield Tennisport. Unfortunately the area didn't develop as expected, and I sold it ten years later.

In the 1960's in one of the professional meetings I met Don Budge. We tried to promote tennis racquets with two inch longer handles. I found a carpenter who extended the handles "that time there was only wooden racquets so it was easy" but none of the tennis equipment companies were interested.

Another tennis adventure was Umpire's chairs which my friend Capek manufactured. The only picture of the chair I have, Pavaroti is sitting on it and arguing with John McEnroe. We were not successful selling many.

Vratislav „Freddie" Botur
s Robertem Redfordem, mezi
herci nejtalentovanějším
tenistou v jeho klubu

NEJZNÁMĚJŠÍ
ČECH V N.Y.

TEXT PAVEL KOVÁŘ REPRO Z RODINNÉHO ARCHIVU

*Cover of Czech Magazine, giving lessons to Robert Redford
(translation: Best known Czech in New York).*

After many years from Sydney meeting Lew Hoad again in New York at exhibition and twenty years later at his Tennis Club in Touremolinos Spain, where the unfortunate Chiang-Er-Shih had a heart attack on the tennis court as described in book.

Trying to sell Kodes, former Wimbledon and Czech Champion, the new plastic tennis court.

Jim Courier, myself, Alex, and Mark Knowles, a Bahamian Champion tennis player.

Pavarotti arguing with John McEnroe for the television commercial sitting on the umpire's chair which was supposed to be our new commercial product.

Virginia Wade and Tony Bennett.

Showing Stan Musial how to grip a tennis racket, instead of a baseball bat.

Steffi Graf and Hanika, two German champions, in the 1980s.

Two top New York Rangers,
avid tennis players.

Sven Davidson, Swedish Davis
Cup player, 1960. Visiting
me at the River Club.

My graduation class celebrating 50th anniversary during the communist year, which I was not able to attend. They have all written me letters admiring my escape, and have all become doctors, professors or writers and I have received wonderful momentos from them. Not many of them now are still alive.

Experimental infrastructure for our tennis courts unsuccessful

Made expressly for Fred Botur by Wilson Sporting Goods Company and very successful in my sales. (Luckily I found the two tennis racquets in the picture in the basement of our house. Today they may be antiques.)

Present from Virginia Wade, a precious and unique
poster with the signatures from all 40 Tennis Champions.
Unfortunately the printing is not clear.

Printed in the United States
by Baker & Taylor Publisher Services